D1145008

Brenda Keyes'

TRADITIONAL SAMPLERS

Herein practise and invention may be free
And as a squirrel skips from tree to tree
So maids may (from their mistresse or their mother)
Learne to leave one worke and to learne another.
For here they may make much choice of which is which
And skip from worke to worke, from stitch to stitch
Until, in time, delightful practise shall
(With profite) make them perfect in them all.
Thus hoping, that these workes may have their guide
To serve for ornament and not for pride:
To cherish virtue, banish idlenesse
For these ends may this book have good successe.

A poem by John Taylor as prefix to 'The Needle's Excellency' 1631.

David & Charles

For my dear father-in-law Jim

ACKNOWLEDGEMENTS

My grateful thanks to the following people for all their help and support:

As ever, my wonderful family, husband Chris, daughter Katie and son Nicholas, for loving me despite my eccentric habit of constantly writing books on embroidery! My mother-in-law Irene for helping to run The Sampler Company. Lindsay Latham for helping with the stitching. My agent Doreen Montgomery for help, advice and constant encouragement. Everyone at David and Charles for their help and expertise especially Cheryl Brown, Brenda Morrison and Jane Trollope. Ethan Danielson for his patience, understanding and total transformation of the preliminary charts. DMC Creative World for fabric and threads. Mike Grey at Framecraft for trinket pots and weddings rings.

A DAVID & CHARLES BOOK

First published in the UK in 1998

A catalogue record for this book is available from the British Library.

ISBN 0 7153 0570 0

Photography by Jon Stewart
Styling by Barbara Stewart
Book design by Anita Ruddell
and printed in Italy by New Interlitho SpA
for David & Charles
Brunel House Newton Abbot Devon

CONTENTS

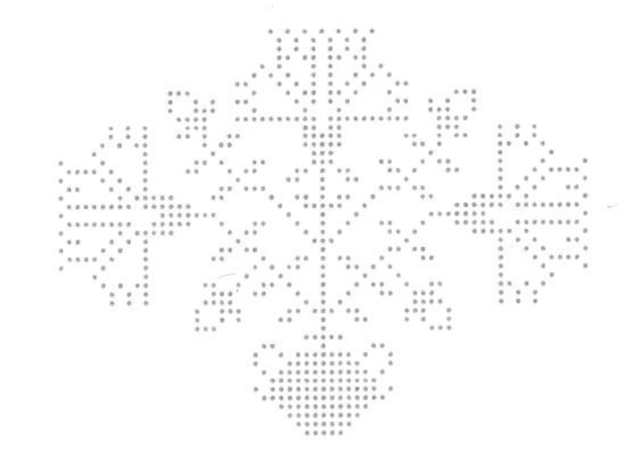

INTRODUCTION

I once heard someone remark that, 'the first piano was made just after there were no pianos'. Although meant as a humorous anecdote, it is the most apt description of the advent of the first sampler. To this day, the earliest known sampler to be signed and dated was worked by Jane Bostocke in 1598, but since we have surviving examples of embroidery from the tombs of the pharaohs, the need to experiment with the shape, composition and art of the stitch, was obviously born long ago.

Detail from Golden Wedding Anniversary Sampler page 78.

Several references to samplers occur much earlier than 1598. The expenses of Elizabeth of York in 1502 recorded the purchase of 'an elne of lynnyn cloth for a sampler for the Queen'. Fifty samplers, recorded for posterity in an inventory of Joan the Mad, Queen of Spain in 1509, worked in silk and gold thread, show how prized they were. The poetry of John Skelton 1460–1529, and the Welsh poet Tudur Aled who died in 1520, contained the word 'sampler' and later William Shakespeare wrote in *Titus Andronicus* (*c*1590):

Fair Philomel, why she but lost her tongue,
And in a tedious sampler sew'd her mind;

Detail from Band Sampler page 16.

The seventeenth century, known as the golden age of sampler making, produced some of the finest samplers ever made. As well as 'spot motif' or 'random' samplers, which featured a variety of motifs stitched at random, the most well known and admired were band samplers. These exquisite and intricately worked pieces were sometimes as long as 40in (102cm), and the work was probably added to over a number of years, as patterns were discovered and recorded.

The first books of printed patterns originating in Europe in the early sixteenth century, were eventually printed in England later in the century. Jacques le Moyne's *La Clef des Champs* was published at Blackfriars in 1586 and contained many patterns for birds, animals and flowers. An

Detail from Susanna Meeks Sampler page 52.

English translation of Frederic di Vinciolo's book *Les Singuliers et Nouveaux Pourtraits pour touttes sortes d'ouvrages di Lingerie* was published in 1591 by John Wolfe with the title of *New and Singular Patterns and workes of Linnen.* This was followed by *A Booke of Curious and Strange Inventions, called the first part of Needleworkes,* published by William Barley in 1596. *The Needle's Excellency,* written and compiled by John Taylor and known to have run to twelve editions by 1640, contained many patterns from Johann Sibmacher's *Schon Neues Modelbuch,* published in 1597. A study of samplers throughout subsequent centuries shows many patterns copied not only from the books themselves, but more often from worked samplers containing the patterns. The original pattern books suffered much wear and tear, in particular the practise of pricking off patterns directly from the page on to the linen.

The influence on eighteenth century sampler designs by imported Indian cottons, with their trailing flower and leaf patterns, cannot be over-estimated. This, together with the fact that linen was much more readily available, brought about great changes, not only to the style of samplers but also their overall shape. Floral borders in particular became less symmetrical, with curved lines and freehand embroidery; and, since the work was no longer rolled up in a workbox, but was thought worthy of display, proportions changed and samplers became almost square in shape.

John Brightland's *Grammar of the English Tongue,* published in 1711 included a 'Sampler Alphabet' in capital letters. By this time, nearly all samplers included at least one alphabet and maybe a verse or inscription. The religious verse or moral tract was prodigious in eighteenth and nineteenth century samplers and it became a firmly established tradition at this time to name and date the work to bear witness to the skill of the worker. This is particularly true of schoolroom samplers, which very often also included the name of the 'dame' (schoolmistress) and school.

DETAIL FROM HESTER BIDDLETON SAMPLER PAGE 48.

The popularity of Berlin woolwork from the 1840s onwards, contributed greatly to the eclipse and virtual decline of the sampler. Its influence can be clearly seen with the elaborate patterns included in late nineteenth century samplers – shepherds, intricately worked flowers and animals, detailed architectural designs of temples, tombs, urns and weeping willows (particularly after the death of Prince Albert in 1861). All signalled a significant style change from earlier sampler design. The major difference, however, was in the materials used, ie, wool on canvas. Examples of Berlin woolwork show that the background fabric (canvas) was worked, as well as the design itself. This was not the case with samplers, where the background canvas was left unworked.

The plain sewing sampler was introduced to schools by the end of the nineteenth century to teach basic sewing skills, but after the First World War with the widespread use of the sewing machine, the art of fine needlework was soon to meet its end. Today, sadly, needlework is not an essential part of the national curriculum. Happily, however, there seems to be a revival of interest in embroidery, due I am sure to an increased awareness of our heritage, a love of antiquities and anything worth preserving for future generations. Auction sales of samplers and antique textiles show that they are now more highly prized than ever. As our generation appreciates the expertise of our forebears in producing these timeless testaments to their talent and dedication, it seems to be producing a desire to add to the tradition, and sampler-making is enjoying an unprecedented revival.

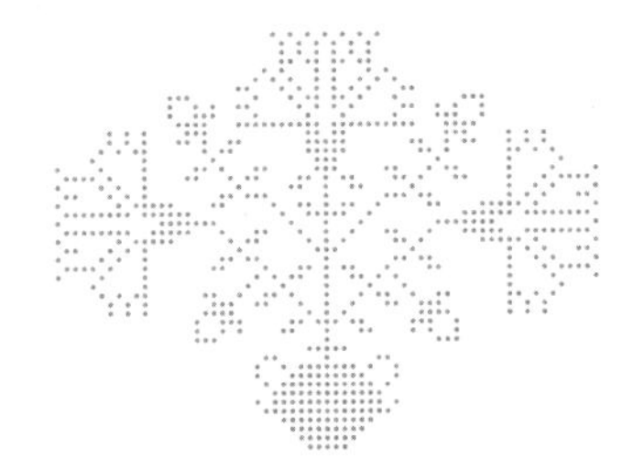

MATERIALS AND EQUIPMENT

Fabrics

As the designs in this book are traditional in nature, linen was the natural choice of fabric for the majority of them. Linen has been the favoured choice of sampler makers for the past four centuries at least, and due to its extreme strength and durability these treasured heirlooms have survived until the present day. If you wish your needlework to not only survive you, but become a treasure of the future, and maybe even one day a museum piece, linen has to be your number one choice. You need not restrict yourself to white, beige or cream however, as a wonderful variety of richly coloured linens are now readily available in many varied counts.

Regarding its supposed difficulty of use, I think it is humbling to remember that girls, some as young as five years of age, worked the most intricate and exquisite samplers on this fabric. The awe-inspiring Bristol Orphanage samplers, many of which survive today, were worked on the finest linen by very young children, thus displaying the skill and delicacy of these young hands.

Aida fabrics, that is fabrics woven in blocks were not used on early samplers but there is no reason, unless you are accurately trying to recreate the look of an antique sampler, not to use them today. I know that purists tend to decry Aida but I feel sure that our ancestors would have welcomed such a fabric with open arms, particularly children or beginners or those with less than perfect eyesight. Since the object of the exercise today is to enjoy our work and not prepare ourselves for a life in service marking household linen, why not make use of what we actually enjoy using? As long as we recognise its limitations, ie, its unsuitability for certain stitches, and use it mainly for cross stitch based designs, we should see it for what it is – a very useful fabric that is easy to use and enjoyable to work on.

Threads

In the past, samplers were worked in silk, wool or cotton, with the occasional addition of silver or gold thread. Nowadays there is a huge variety of threads to choose from – Flower thread, Marlitt viscose thread, perlé cotton, metallics etc. There is certainly no need to limit your choice to stranded cotton (floss). Wonderful effects can be achieved by substituting different threads. A word of caution here though, if you are aiming for a totally traditional look, the use of, say, a space-dyed or variegated thread would be inappropriate. This type of thread adds a wonderful new dimension to work with a more modern feel and you will see examples of its use throughout the book.

Using space-dyed or variegated thread

When using variegated thread (so called because the colour gradually changes from a very pale to a darker shade of the same colour), it is important to select the lengths carefully to ensure that the change of colour is gradual throughout your stitching – that is, avoid placing dark thread directly next to light. Beautifully subtle effects can be achieved in your embroidery as the colours merge and the shades vary. On the other hand, some space-dyed threads are dyed with sudden and dramatic changes of colour at quite short intervals, giving a totally different look. For both types of thread, if you are working in cross stitch, it is important to complete each cross individually, and not work a line of half crosses and then complete by working back along the line.

Needles

For the projects in this book, you will need blunt-ended (tapestry) needles in sizes 20, 24 and 26. Use size 20 for the canvas work projects, the cushion and pincushion, size 26 for the fine linen 28–36 count; and size 24 for 25 count linen. I

always find it useful to keep a large stock of needles as it is so frustrating not to have the appropriate one to hand when beginning a project.

Hoops and Frames

Using a hoop, a frame, or simply holding the stitching in your hand, is a matter of personal choice. There is a school of thought that says more even stitching is obtained with the use of a frame, that the work stays cleaner and retains its crisp finish (and I personally go along with this), but if you find either a hoop or a frame awkward to use, then your stitching will be an unhappy affair and this will show in the finished work.

If you decide to use an embroidery hoop, always use one that is big enough to house the complete design (though this obviously restricts the use to smaller projects). This will ensure that the hoop never needs to be placed over any stitching and will not spoil the completed work with pulled and snagged stitches. To prevent your fabric slipping about, and also to protect it from the wood, it is advisable to bind both the inner and outer hoops with white bias binding secured with a few stitches. Another way to protect your work from hoop marks is to place a piece of tissue paper between the fabric and the hoop, then tear away the middle section to expose the area to be worked. Remember to remove your hoop every time you finish working.

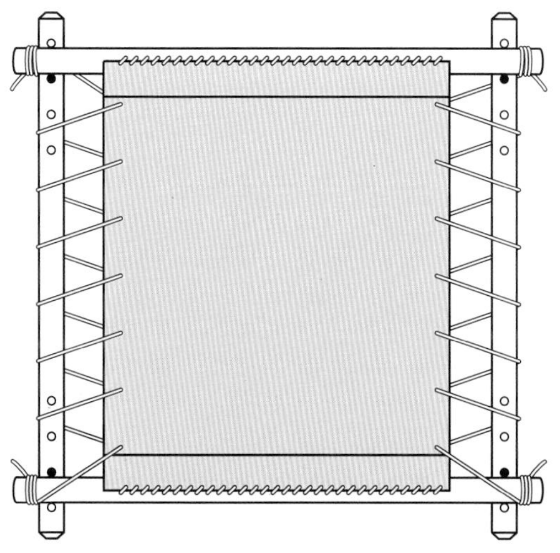

Fig 1 Lacing the fabric into the frame.

Larger pieces of work will require a rectangular frame. These come in many sizes and are particularly useful when working in tent stitch which tends to distort fabric. First strengthen the edges of your fabric by hemming or binding with tape. Then, sew the top and bottom edges of the fabric to the webbing which is attached to the rollers of the frame. It is important to ensure that the fabric is placed evenly in the frame – if attached unevenly it will become distorted. Assemble the frame and lace the side edges of the fabric to the stretchers with very strong thread (see Fig 1).

A quicker and easier, though just as effective, way of keeping your fabric taut is to use an interlocking bar frame made from either plastic or wood (see Suppliers page 143). These can be purchased individually or in multi-packs which enable you to make up many different sized square and rectangular frames. I feel these frames have many advantages – there are no protruding corners to catch your thread on, they are extremely light to hold, easier to store and more portable.

Adhesives

For some of the projects you will need to use glue, for example the covered mount for the Little Girls Birth Sampler on page 126. There are many adhesives available, but I always prefer to use UHU glue. I have had good results with this product which is recommended for use with fabric and dries on impact. Another major point in its favour, is that the fumes associated with this type of product are far less obvious with this brand.

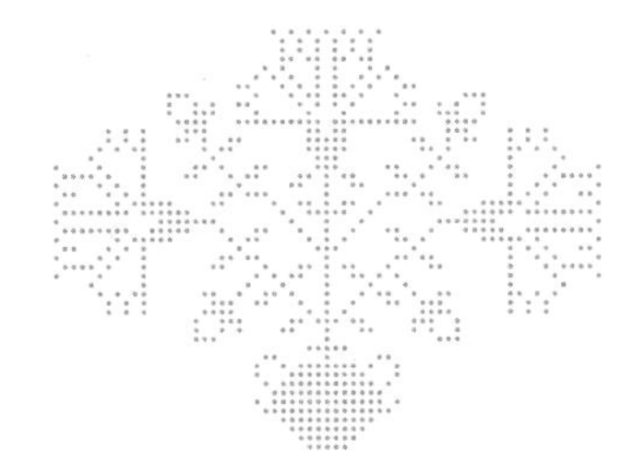

WORKBOX

How to Read a Chart

The method for 'translating' all counted needlework charts is the same – whether they be hand drawn or computer generated, containing black and white symbols, colour blocks or colour symbols. One square on the chart, containing a symbol or colour represents one stitch (usually a cross stitch) on your fabric. The instructions given with each particular design will tell you how many threads of fabric to work over. Fig 2 shows clearly how the chart has been 'translated' on to the fabric. The blank squares mean that this area is left unworked unless otherwise stated (for example if the background was to be filled with a single colour). Straight black lines surrounding a motif indicate backstitch. Traditionally, motifs were seldom outlined in backstitch and you will usually only see this method employed on more modern samplers or embroidery designs.

Fig 2 The chart 'translated' onto the fabric.

You will see that some of the projects have two charts – one for the design motifs and another for the verse or lettering. They are charted separately because the two elements are worked over different numbers of fabric threads. In these cases the first letter of each line is also charted on the main chart to help you position the words correctly. Some charts (eg page 128) have a ruled line or lines to indicate where the lettering of your choice is to be placed. This line is not stitched.

The star symbol on the charts indicates the centre of the chart, to help with positioning on the fabric when starting to stitch.

Enlarging and Reducing Charted Designs

Charted designs are extremely versatile and very easy to enlarge or reduce. The following suggestions should help you achieve this and enjoy all the designs shown regardless of their intricacy.

❊ If you find the fabric threads difficult to see, simply change the thread count of the suggested fabric to one you are happy working with. For example, a design with a stitch count of 96 x 96 worked over one thread of Belfast linen with 32 threads per inch (2.5cm), will have a finished size of 3 x 3in (8 x 8cm). The same design worked on Dublin linen with 25 threads per inch (2.5cm) is much easier to see and will be 4 x 4in (10 x 10cm) in size. Not a huge increase but worth it if it means you can actually enjoy stitching a design you would otherwise have been unable to.

❊ If your eyesight is not the problem but you wish to increase the size of a design to use for another purpose, say turning a small picture into a cushion, try working the stitches over two, three or even four threads or blocks of fabric. For example, if you work over four threads instead of two, the design will double in size. Likewise, if the instructions state that the design is worked in cross stitch over two threads of linen and you work over just one thread in cross stitch or tent stitch, the design size will be halved.

✻ Consider every square in the design to be two, three or even four stitches square instead of one. For example, to triple the design size, work a block of stitches three by three for every one stitch shown.

Stitching from a Large Chart

If you have easy access to a photocopier, photocopy the chart, enlarging if necessary, then cut this chart into workable sections – the alphabet for example. If you are working on a frame you can then simply pin or tack (baste) the relevant section of the chart conveniently near to the area to be stitched. I have found that this saves a great deal of time and eliminates the problem of where best to place your chart for easy stitching.

Finding the Centre of the Fabric

Most instructions suggest that you begin work at the centre of the fabric, to ensure that your work is placed centrally, avoiding the horrible possibility of working off the edge of the fabric. To find the centre, fold your fabric in half and half again and crease lightly. Tack (baste) along these lines in a contrasting sewing thread. The centre of the fabric is where the lines cross. If, however, you want to start work at, say, the top left-hand corner of the design (and this often seems to be a more logical alternative with designs that include a border, samplers in particular), you must calculate carefully where to start stitching by deducting the design size from your fabric size and positioning accordingly. For example, if your fabric size is 12 x 10in (30.5 x 25.5cm) and your design size 8 x 6in (20.5 x 15cm) you will have 4in (10cm) of spare fabric. You should therefore measure 2in (5cm) down from the top edge and 2in (5cm) in from the side edge and begin work here.

Starting to Stitch

The following advice will help to achieve perfect stitching.

Cut your thread into lengths no longer than 12–18in (30.5–46cm), 12in (30.5cm) maximum for metallic thread. Many stitchers make the mistake of thinking that if they use longer lengths, it will save time constantly re-threading needles. What actually happens, is that the thread tangles more easily and stitching can take even longer. Thread also loses its lustre in the process of being pulled back and forward through the fabric and the end of a long length can become very tired looking.

When using stranded cotton (floss) always separate and untwist all six strands before selecting the number of strands required. The amount will depend not only on the fabric used, but also the tension of your stitch. I stitch with quite a loose tension, so that in general two strands will give adequate coverage on, say, 28 count linen. Someone who stitches with a tighter stitch, may consider using three strands. If you are new to stitching, it would be a good idea to experiment with a small piece of the fabric you intend to use and varying numbers of strands. It really is worth going to the trouble of untwisting and recombining your threads, as they will lie flatter and give greater coverage. Some stitchers go to even greater lengths to ensure perfection and employ a technique called 'railroading'. This involves using the needle to separate the strands of cotton as the stitch is completed to ensure they are not twisted.

Never use a knot to begin stitching. Knots can pull through the fabric and will give a bumpy finish which will spoil the appearance of your work. To begin stitching previously unworked fabric, bring the needle up through the fabric leaving about 1in (2.5cm) of thread at the back. Holding the thread in place, work three or four stitches until the trailing thread is caught and secured (Fig 3). To begin a new thread on fabric which has

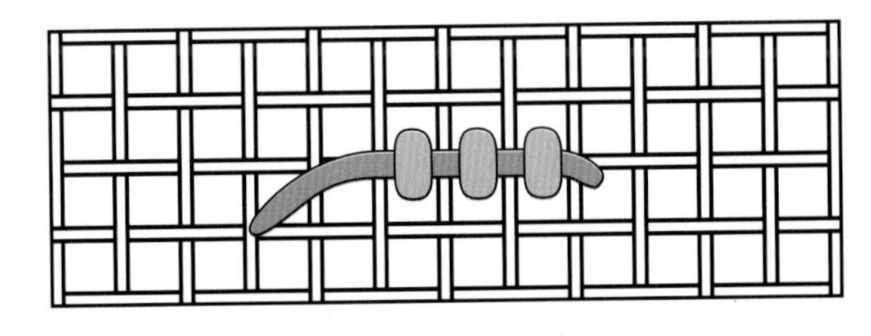

Fig 3 Starting to stitch.

been previously stitched, simply run the needle through the loops of three or four stitches at the back of the work near to where you wish to begin stitching. Bring the needle up at the required place and begin. Be careful not to pull the stitches too tightly; they should sit evenly on the fabric.

To ensure a smooth, even finish to your work, make sure that all top stitches lie in the same direction – it does not matter if this is top left to bottom right or top right to bottom left. A helpful reminder is to work a stitch quite a bit larger than your other stitches in the direction you have chosen for your top stitch, in a corner of the fabric for reference. Remember to 'drop' your needle every four or five stitches as this will take the twist out of the thread and avoid tangles.

Finishing Off

The method for finishing and securing a thread is much the same as starting. Leaving yourself enough thread to finish, take the needle through to the back of the work. Run the needle through the back loop of three or four stitches and snip off the thread close to the stitching (Fig 4).

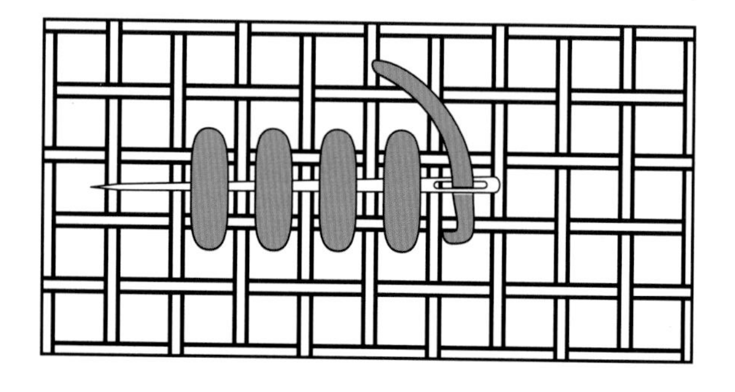

Fig 4 Finishing off a thread.

Embroidery (unless it has become very grubby in the working) always looks better if it hasn't been washed or ironed. Employing the following simple measures will avoid such an eventuality.

❊ Always wash your hands before starting to sew.

❊ Store your work in a clean, white pillowcase, or if too big, wrap in a clean white cloth.

❊ Try and dissuade admiring onlookers from running their fingers over your work. Beautiful embroidery seems to bring about a compulsion to do this!

❊ Avoid potential disaster by never drinking tea, coffee or other hazardous liquids near your work.

Ageing Your Work

Firstly, I must state the obvious, that your work will in time mellow and age to that lovely soft, old look you probably love in antique samplers. If you simply cannot wait for time to take its course, it is possible to 'age' your work. The most well-known method (beloved by BBC costume drama departments), is tea or coffee dyeing (more usually tea). There are two ways to do this and unless you are completely fearless, I would advise the former.

Method 1

Make a pot of strong tea using tea bags. Half fill a large bowl with tepid water and pour the tea into it. Place your chosen fabric and threads (having first removed the paper bands from the threads) into the liquid and squeeze gently so that they absorb the colour. When the fabric and threads have begun to take on the colour, take out and lay on several sheets of blotting paper (or an old towel). When you have achieved the desired effect, leave to dry. The fabric and threads should now have faded down to more subtle shades. If you wish them to be even darker, repeat the process with a stronger brew.

This method enables you to use the fabric and threads if you like the results of the dye, or discard them if you don't. Although expensive (if you choose to discard them), this method will cause less heartbreak than if you follow method 2. Another similar method I have had great success with, is to simply dye the fabric and then choose subtly coloured shades.

Method 2

This is basically the same as the above method, but is undertaken *after* you have finished your embroidery (like I said, not for the fainthearted!). Dylon have produced a cold-water dye, colour Koala Brown, and a very helpful instruction leaflet which will advise you on how to achieve a similar effect.

Labelling Your Work

This may seem a rather odd suggestion, but if you are working one of the reproduction samplers and wish to keep the original date, it is important to record the actual date that the sampler was stitched and by whom. You may even like to include further information – precise details of linen and threads used for example, your place of birth, address, whether the sampler was a gift, and for what occasion. This will do much to avoid confusion in the future – perhaps two to three hundred years time. Imagine if you will, an enthusiastic sampler collector pondering upon the puzzling occurrence of a sampler stitched on Aida fabric and dated 1832! I would suggest either a sticky label firmly adhered to the back of the frame, or a small card (about the size of a gift card) inserted between the work and the backing card. Not only will this provide clear and concise information, it will make for very interesting reading and provide an insight into the stitching habits of our generation.

Beadwork

Beadwork is an easy technique to master and once learned will bring added interest to your work. Beads can be substituted for stranded cotton (floss) for some of the motifs in a design, working particularly well with fruit motifs. Beads added to a border will also bring an extra dimension. A beadwork chart looks the same as a counted needlework chart, but the squares represent beads instead of stitches. You will need to use a beading needle with a very narrow eye which is able to pass easily through the bead. Match your sewing thread to the colour of the fabric. Polyester sewing thread is a good choice as it is strong and thin, but if you are stitching lots of beads to your work, it is best to use quilting thread which is even stronger and will hold the beads more securely. If you are only adding a few beads, simply use one strand of the stranded cotton (floss) you are stitching with.

The beads are usually attached with a half cross stitch. However, if you are working on quite a large piece, tent stitch is a better option as it will hold the beads more securely so that they don't sag on the fabric. Bring your needle up through the fabric as you would for a half cross stitch. Thread the bead onto the needle (you will probably find it easier to pick up the bead by 'stabbing' it with the needle itself rather than using your fingers), and insert it into the fabric, completing the stitch. Bring the needle up for the next stitch in the same way and continue.

Avoiding and Rectifying Mistakes

For sampler making in particular, the most common mistake seems to be the 'border that doesn't meet'. For the uninitiated, this is the horrible consequence of miscounting stitches and finding that the final coming together of the border design doesn't. There are several easy ways to avoid this distressing occurrence.

❋ Work lines of tacking (basting) stitches vertically and horizontally, and then draw a pencil line on your chart in the same position. This will aid placement of stitches. For the border in particular however, check the stitch count of the design and work a line of tacking (basting) stitches one row outside the edge of the border. This preparation will take only minutes, but will aid accuracy and avoid much tearing out of hair (and stitches).

❋ Resolve to count, count and count again. I find myself adopting a sing-song tone of 3 up 3 down, 5 across, 3 up 3 down, 5 across when working a border and it really helps.

❋ Stop at the end of every length of thread and check that all is well. This will avoid big mistakes.

✻ When working a symmetrical border, check that motifs or lines of stitches are correctly placed by constantly checking across the fabric to see they lie in the same position horizontally and vertically.

If you do make a mistake however and have to unpick a section of your work, the following tips should help avoid catastrophe.

✻ If it is a big mistake, take a deep breath, remain calm, leave the scene of the accident and go and make a reviving cup of tea or coffee.

✻ Using sharp embroidery scissors, snip through every cross stitch (or whatever stitch you have been working in). This will ensure that you are not dragging long lengths of thread through the fabric, pulling and distorting it unnecessarily. Unpick the stitches carefully.

✻ You may find that no matter how carefully you unpick your stitches, you are left with an 'imprint' of the work. Try gently rubbing the affected area with a piece of fabric the same colour as the base fabric of the design. This will usually dislodge the tiny fibres and remove them. You could also try pressing a small piece of masking tape onto the fibres and lifting it off. The fibres should stick to the masking tape. I would urge caution here however. The last thing you want is a nasty sticky mess instead of a few stray fibres.

✻ Now that you have removed all the errant thread, you will almost certainly find that the threads of the base fabric have been pulled out of shape. You now need to re-align them. The way to do this is to take a blunt tapestry needle and carefully draw it down the fabric in between the threads. This should restore them to their former position.

✻ If you are designing your own work and simply change your mind about, for example, the placement of a motif, try to design over the unpicked area as this will eliminate all mistakes completely.

STITCH LIBRARY

Almost all the projects in this book are worked with stitches that can be classified as 'counted thread' stitches. Stitch diagrams are given for all of them, but as an added tip, take care when working tent stitch over one thread of fabric not to pull the stitch too tightly, as this will result in the embroidery thread slipping behind the warp thread of the fabric.

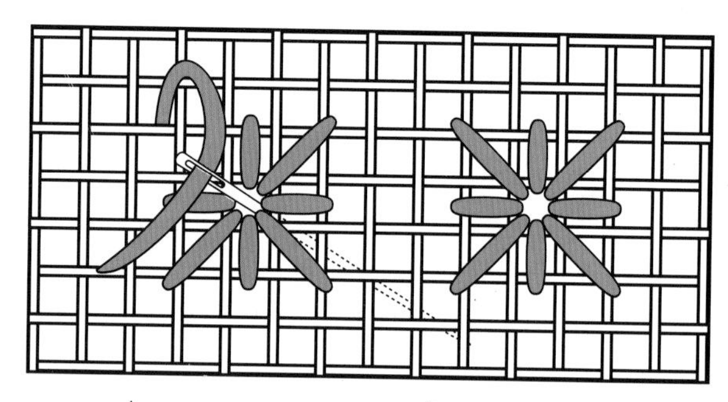

Algerian eye stitch (Eyelet stitch)

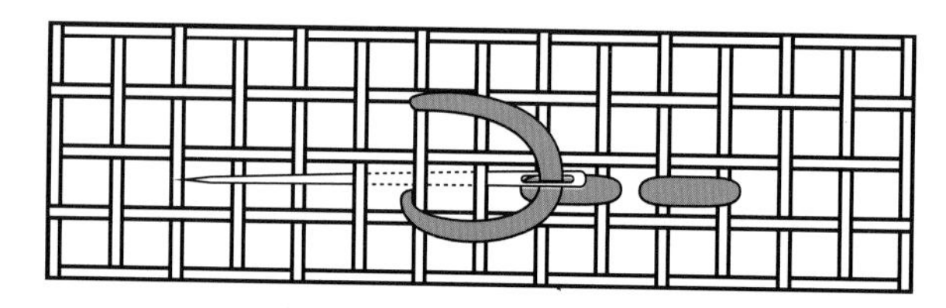

Backstitch

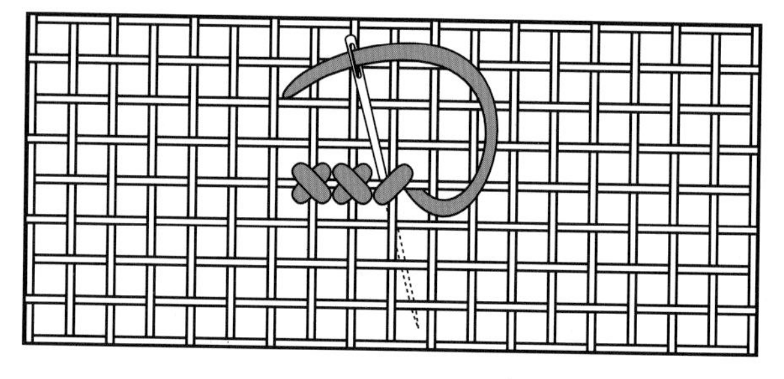

Cross stitch over one thread

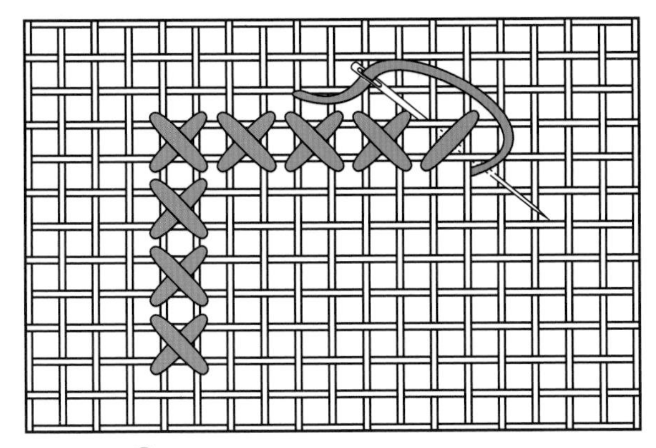

Cross stitch over two threads

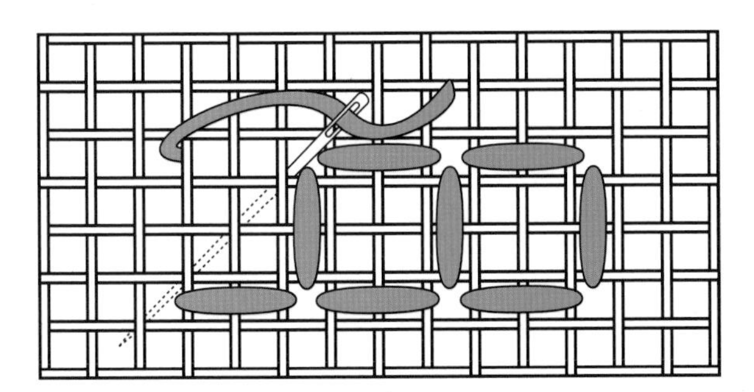

Four-sided stitch

Pulled thread stitch
(satin stitch pulled tight)

Padded cross stitch
(work a cross stitch, then another on top)

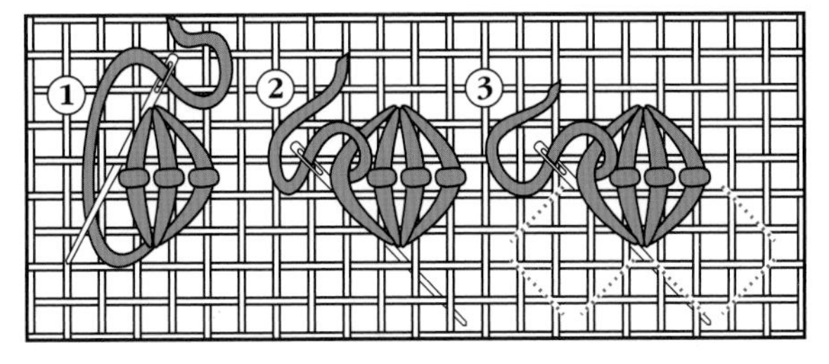

Queen stitch

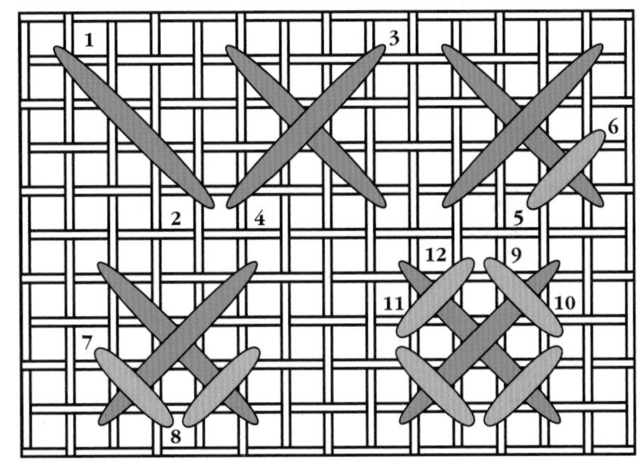

Rice stitch

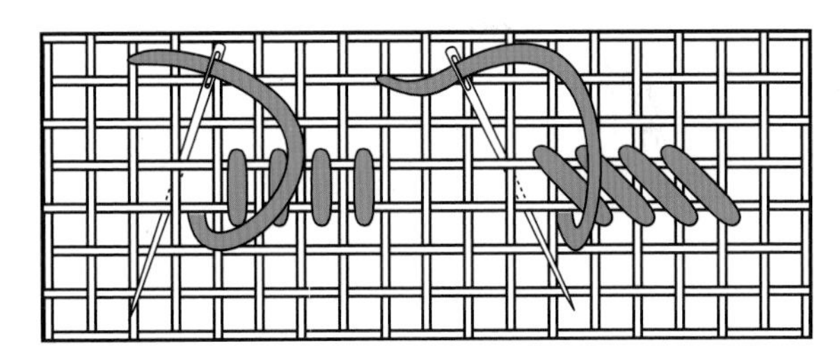

Satin stitch

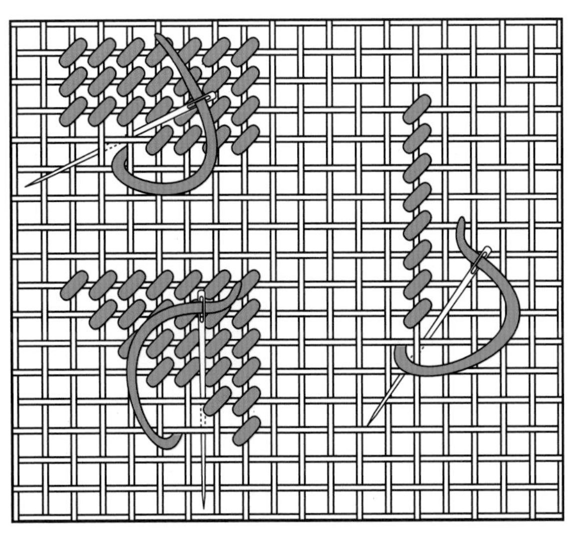

Tent stitch

Mary Elizabeth Nicholson
1892
There is a path that leads to truth
Some may go astray
Narrow but pleasant is the road
And wise men love the way
Margaret Simcock
Aged 9 1848
Behold how good and how pleasant it is for
brethren to dwell together in unity.
Hannah Richards Aged 11 1886
H.R.

REPRODUCTION SAMPLERS

For those who would dearly love to own an antique sampler but are put off by the ever increasing prices, a reproduction sampler is the answer. Of the four samplers in this chapter, three are reproduced entirely from the originals in my own collection – Margaret Simcock, Mary Elizabeth Nicholson and Hannah Richards. The Band Sampler is worked in the style of a seventeenth century original. I have added suggestions in the Workbox section (page 10) regarding the practices of ageing and labelling your work – practices particularly pertinent to this chapter. Some people believe that it is unethical to work a sampler complete with the original date, as this could cause much confusion in centuries to come. Some even believe it to be an out-and-out forgery!

My own view is that throughout time artisans and craftsmen have enjoyed working copies of original masterpieces, whether they be paintings, sculptures, pieces of furniture, or even china ornaments. So why not samplers? The main objection is the adding of the original date, but since the majority of samplers had a date very much in evidence, the finished work would not look authentic without it. My solution is to include as much written information as possible with every sampler worked, but in particular with reproduction samplers. This includes the actual date the work was finished, the worker's name, age, address, materials used, and even the reason for working the sampler. This information could then be either affixed to the back of the frame, or, to ensure its longevity, placed inside the frame itself, between the embroidery and the backing board. Future generations will I'm sure be fascinated to learn of our stitching habits and be grateful that we have taken the time and trouble to record the details of our craft so thoroughly.

Band Sampler

The seventeenth century has been described as the golden age of sampler making and the best known and loved of all seventeenth century samplers are band samplers. These exquisitely executed examples usually consisted of rows of border patterns interspersed with alphabets and occasionally a verse or poem. Some of the text is difficult to read, as the worker would not trouble to fit the words into the line, but simply ended a word at the margin, beginning the next line with the remainder of it. This particular version, worked in pastel shades, contains a wide variety of stitches and patterns used in the seventeenth century – cross, four-sided, satin, rice, Algerian eye and queen stitch.

DESIGN SIZE: 7 X 24IN (18 X 61CM)
STITCH COUNT: 109 X 372

❋ 12 x 29in (30.5 x 74cm) cream Belfast linen, 32 threads per inch (2.5cm)

❋ Stranded cottons (floss) as shown in the key

❋ Use two strands of stranded cotton (floss) over two threads of linen, unless otherwise indicated in the key.

The charts on pages 18–21 have numbered rows from 1 to 18, which refer to specific stitches. As you reach each row, follow the instructions with the relevant expanded stitch diagrams, referring also to the Stitch Library on page 12.

To work the verse, follow the chart on page 21, working with one strand 926 slate blue stranded cotton (floss) over one thread. The first letter of each row is also charted on the main chart on page 19 to help you position the verse correctly. The rows are underlined by a pink running stitch.

1 Measure 3in (8cm) down from the top of the fabric, and 3in (8cm) in from the left-hand side and begin here in cross stitch following the chart.

2 To personalise the sampler, work out names, dates etc using the alphabets given, in pencil on graph paper and position on the dotted line shown on the chart.

3 Stretch, mount and frame as required (see pages 137–139 for advice).

ABCDEFGHIJKLMNO
PQRSTUVWXYZ
abcdefghijklmnopqrstu
vwxyz 1234567890
ABCDEFGHIJKL
OPQRSTUVWXYZ
Not Land but Learning Makes a Man complete
Not Birth but breeding Makes him truly great
Brenda Keyes 1998

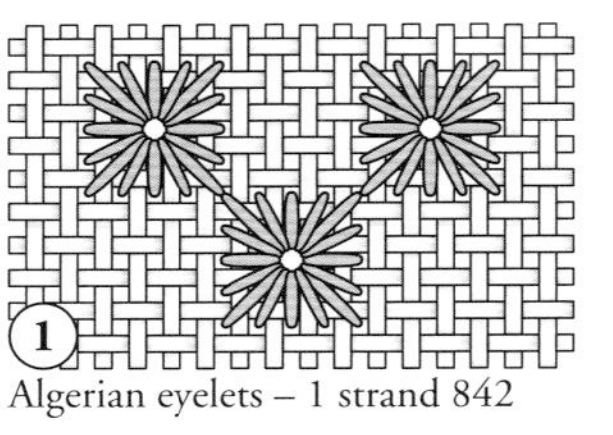

Algerian eyelets – 1 strand 842

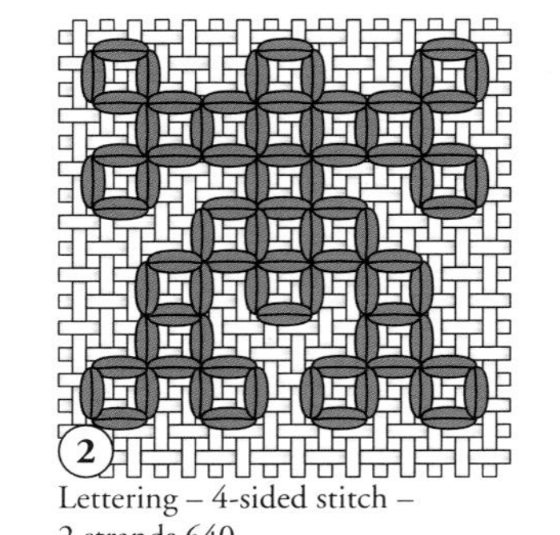

Lettering – 4-sided stitch –
2 strands 640

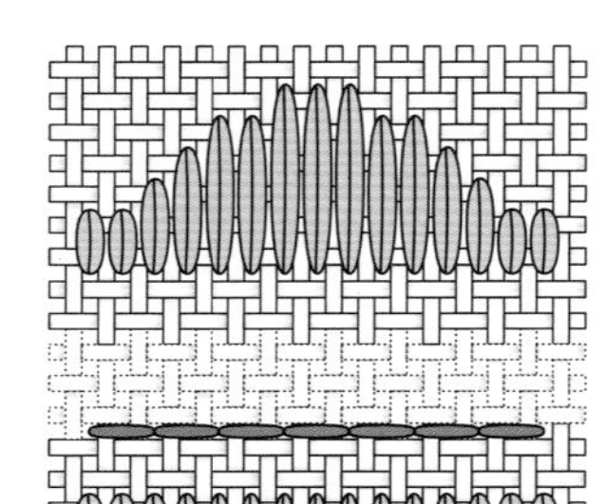
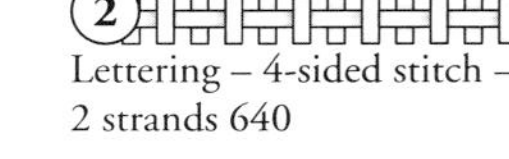

Satin stitch – 2 strands 842

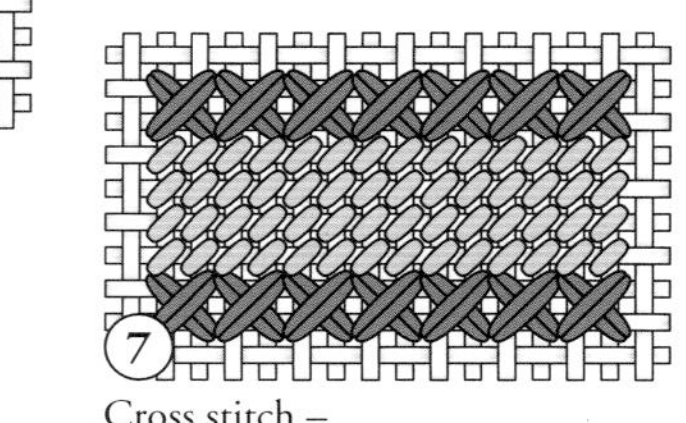

Rice stitch – over 4 threads
2 strands 407 + 1 strand 842

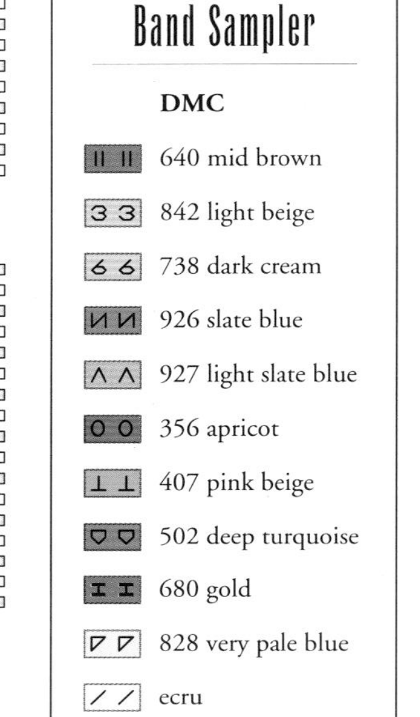

Band Sampler

DMC

- 640 mid brown
- 842 light beige
- 738 dark cream
- 926 slate blue
- 927 light slate blue
- 356 apricot
- 407 pink beige
- 502 deep turquoise
- 680 gold
- 828 very pale blue
- ecru

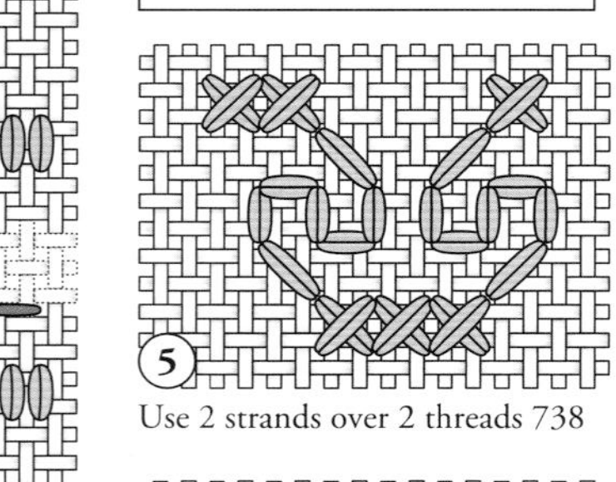

Use 2 strands over 2 threads 738

Use 1 strand 828 + 407

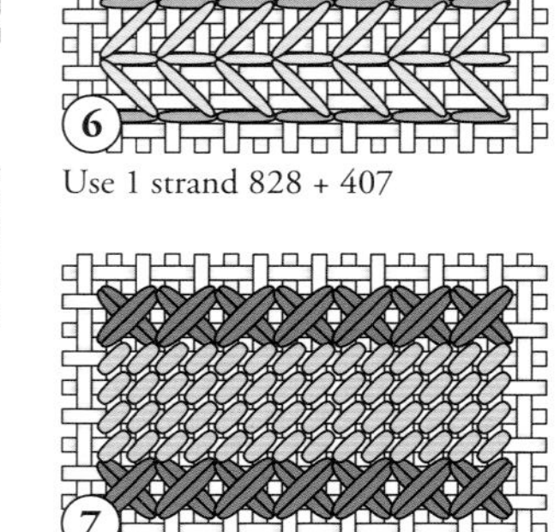

Cross stitch –
2 strands over 2 threads 640
Tent stitch –
2 strands over 1 thread 842

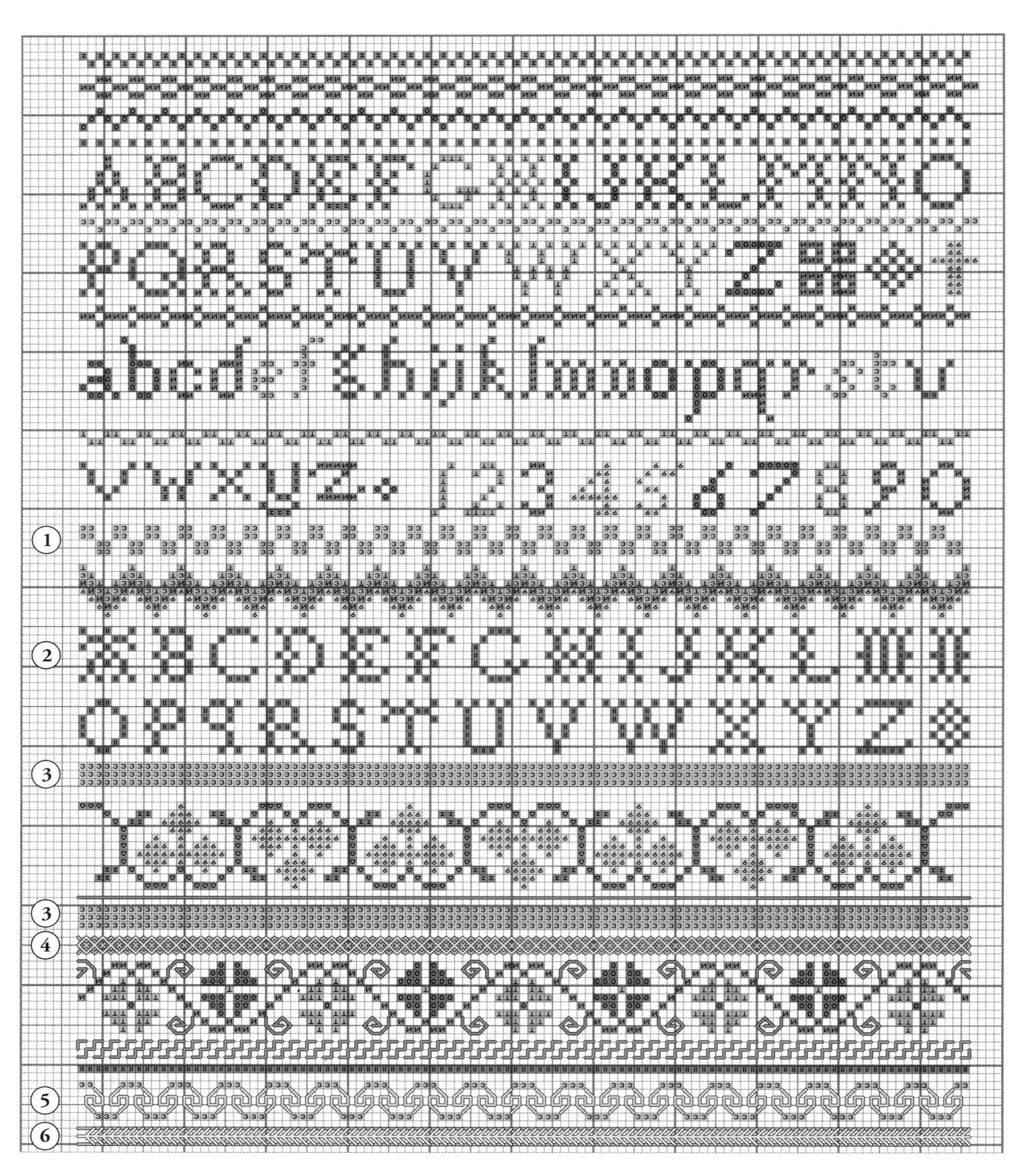

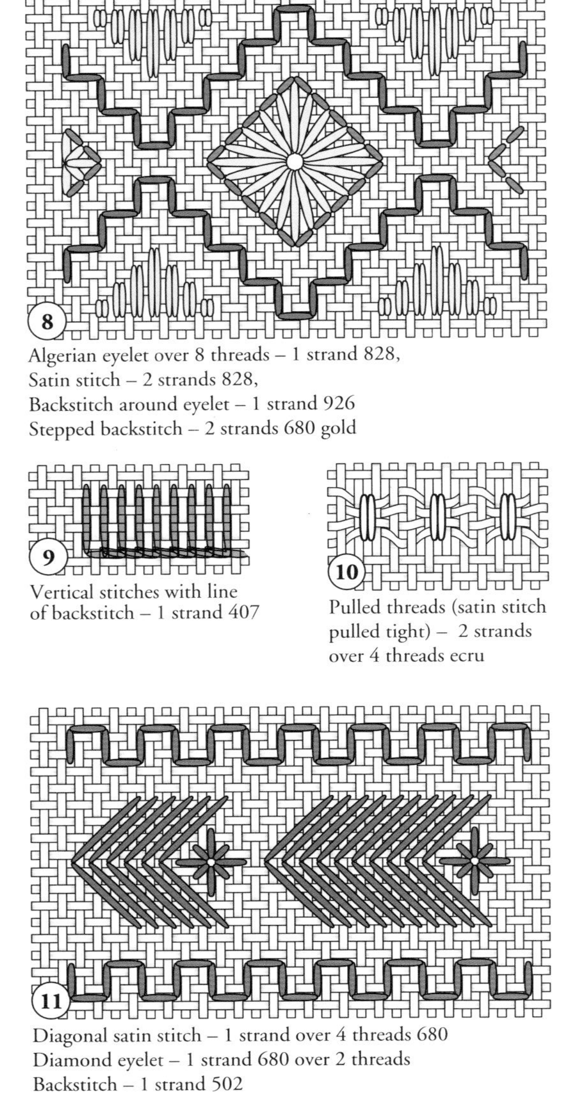

Algerian eyelet over 8 threads – 1 strand 828,
Satin stitch – 2 strands 828,
Backstitch around eyelet – 1 strand 926
Stepped backstitch – 2 strands 680 gold

Vertical stitches with line of backstitch – 1 strand 407

Pulled threads (satin stitch pulled tight) – 2 strands over 4 threads ecru

Diagonal satin stitch – 1 strand over 4 threads 680
Diamond eyelet – 1 strand 680 over 2 threads
Backstitch – 1 strand 502

Satin stitch – 2 strands 738

Small eyelet – 1 strand 640

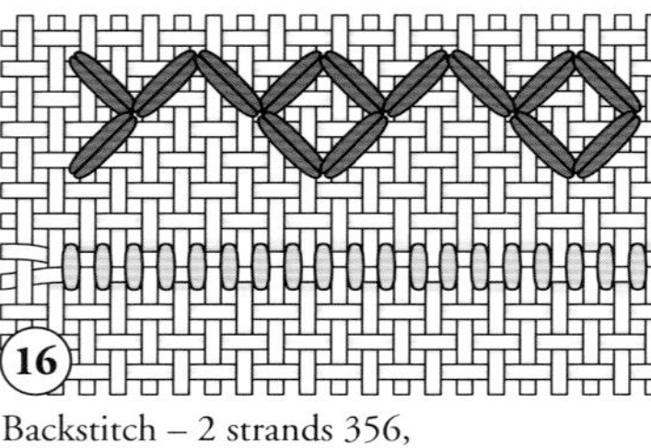

16 Backstitch – 2 strands 356,
Pulled stitch (satin stitch pulled tight) –
1 strand over 2 threads 738

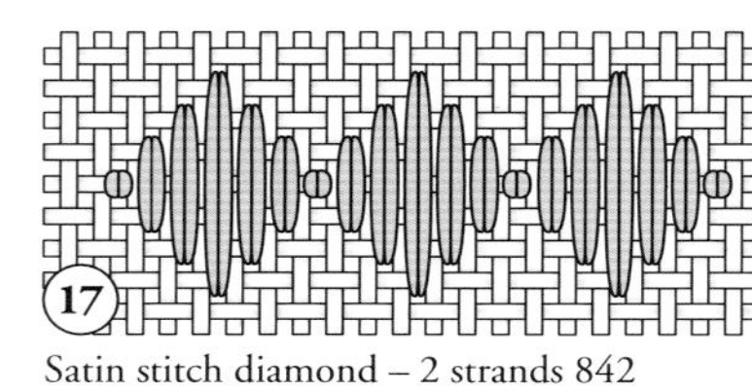

17 Satin stitch diamond – 2 strands 842

18 Pulled threads (satin stitch pulled tight) –
2 strands over 4 threads ecru

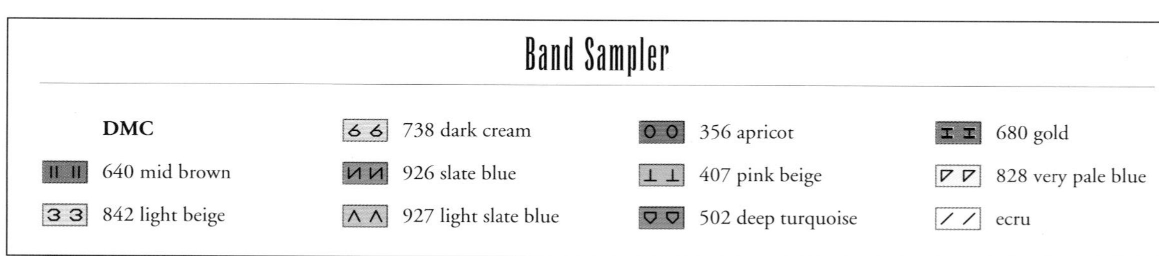

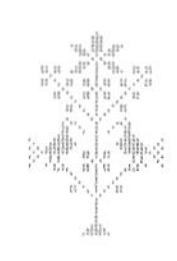

Bargello using 2 strands (matching colours with key), and blackwork using 1 strand 640

Queen stitch using 1 strand 842, 407 and 356, with backstitches using 2 strands 680, Algerian eyelet and backstitches using 2 strand 738

Lettering – cross stitch over 1 thread using 1 strand 926 slate blue

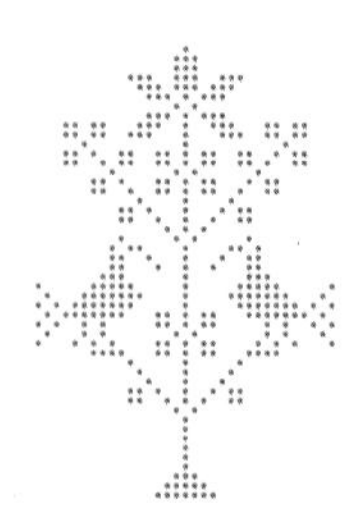

The Margaret Simcock Sampler

This reproduction of the original Margaret Simcock sampler would be an ideal choice for a beginner or intermediate stitcher. Worked in subtle shades of pink, brown and green, the sampler is typical of its period with its berry border and dominating manor house. Houses were a popular choice for sampler makers of the mid-nineteenth century and the same house often appears on several samplers from the same area. Symbolically, the rose is seen to represent love, patience and beauty. The very young Margaret Simcock seems to have embodied all three in her delightful sampler.

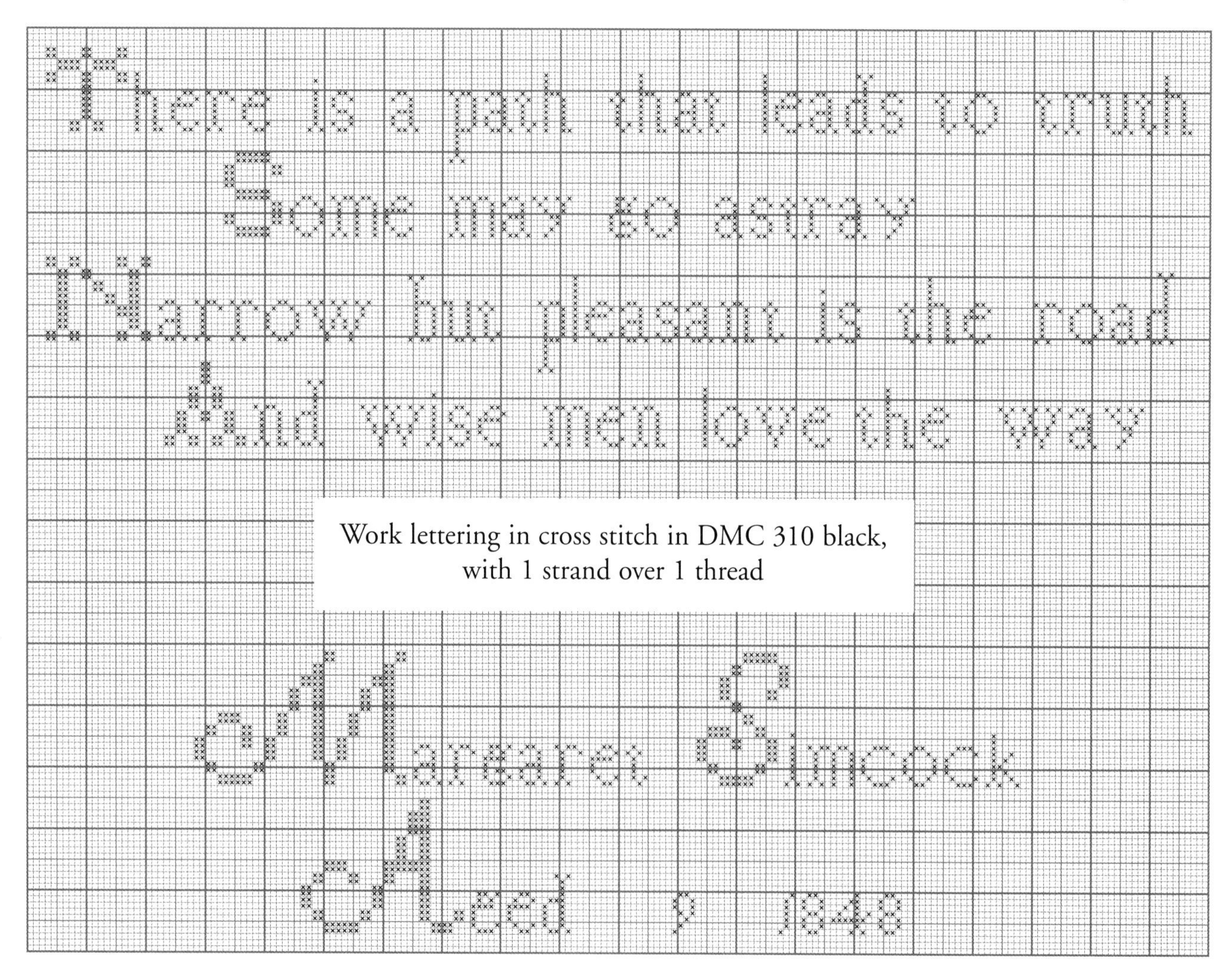

Work lettering in cross stitch in DMC 310 black, with 1 strand over 1 thread

There is a path that leads to truth
Some may go astray
Narrow but pleasant is the road
And wise men love the way
Margaret Simcock
Aged 9 1848

DESIGN SIZE: 14 X 14IN (35.5 X 35.5CM)
STITCH COUNT: 197 X 197

❊ 18 x 18in (46 x 46cm) cream evenweave linen, 28 threads per inch (2.5cm). The linen for this sampler was dyed with Dylon's Koala Brown, following the manufacturer's instructions.

❊ Stranded cottons (floss) as shown in the key

❊ Use two strands of stranded cotton (floss) over two threads of linen, except for the lower case section of the verse, name, age and date, which is worked with one strand over one thread. To work the lettering, follow the chart on page 22. The first letter of each row is also charted on the main chart here to help you position the verse correctly.

1 Find the centre of the design and work outwards in cross stitch from this point following the chart.

2 Stretch, mount and frame as required (see pages 137–139 for advice).

Margaret Simcock Sampler

DMC

Symbol	Colour	Symbol	Colour
→ →	371 mid sage	+ +	223 deep pink
3 3	842 flesh	ǁ ǁ	3772 deep pink brown
⊥ ⊥	407 pink beige	K K	927 light slate blue
– –	ecru	\\ \\	3782 grey brown
X X	310 black	▬ ▬	3053 light green grey

Text – 310 black
use 1 strand over 1 thread

The Hannah Richards Sampler

This design is a smaller version of the original which was worked in wool on canvas. Hannah Richards worked her sampler very much in the style of the period (in the original, the verse was much longer, taking up almost a third of the design). The alphabets, borders and motifs are all typical of the time and it is clear that Hannah based her design around the home, and things she saw every day. It is intriguing to wonder if the little figure with the stick is her father, the dog, her dog; and if the row of black crows ending with one brown crow was deliberate, or if she simply ran out of black thread!

Design size: 15 x 11¼in (38 x 29cm)
Stitch count: 227 x 172

❋ 19 x 16in (48 x 40.5cm) unbleached linen, 28 threads per inch (2.5cm)

❋ Stranded cottons (floss) as shown in the key

❋ Use two strands of stranded cotton (floss) over two threads of linen.

1 Find the centre of the design and work outwards in cross stitch from this point following the chart. The large alphabet is worked in Algerian eye stitch (see Stitch Library page 12).

2 To substitute a name, age or date, work out your details in pencil on graph paper, using alphabets and numerals from the additional alphabets on page 135, and position as shown on the chart.

3 Stretch, mount and frame as required (see pages 137–139 for advice).

Wool on Canvas

Many late-nineteenth century samplers were worked with wool on canvas, due in the main to the huge popularity of Berlin woolwork, and thus the ready availability of materials. It is lamentable that the Victorians made this choice, as it seems to have signalled the end of exquisite sampler making as we have come to recognise it. Although cross stitch was certainly the number one choice for sampler makers across the centuries (so much so that it became known as 'sampler stitch'), the advent of canvas as a base fabric for samplers all but eliminated experimentation with other stitches.

Behold how good and how pleasant it is for
brethren to dwell together in unity.
Hannah Richards Aged 11
1886
H.R.
AIGUILLES

Behold how good and how pl
brethren to dwell together
Hannah Richards Aged

Hannah Richards Sampler

DMC

- 310 black
- ecru
- 3753 very pale blue
- 322 mid blue
- 902 maroon
- 921 deep orange
- 890 dark green
- 300 chocolate brown
- 730 sage green
- 407 flesh (for face)

The Mary Elizabeth Nicholson Sampler

Originally worked in wool on canvas, this rich Victorian floral design of bright colours and unusual geometric border is probably of Welsh origin. Detailed motifs such as the figures were taken from Berlin woolwork patterns of the time, and are hugely different to the often stick-like figures previously featured on samplers. Colours were also influenced by woolwork, and were even brighter than the silks and cottons used on linen. Mary's sampler, finished in 1892, is one of the more interesting from the period. By the end of the nineteenth century, samplers were dying out in popularity, and were sometimes sad, simple offerings with little flair. Happily, Mary worked with a love of the art which shines through.

Design size: 17¾ x 17¾in (45 x 45cm)
Stitch count: 225 x 225

* 22 x 22in (56 x 56cm) cream Dublin linen, 25 threads per inch (2.5cm)

* Stranded cottons (floss) as shown in the key

* Use two strands of stranded cotton (floss) over two threads of linen throughout.

1 Find the centre of the design and work outwards in cross stitch following the chart.

2 If you wish to substitute a name or date, work out your details in pencil on graph paper using the alphabet and numerals given here, and then position as shown on the chart.

3 Stretch, mount and frame as required (see pages 137–139 for advice).

Crowns and Coronets

The crown or coronet was widely used in Tudor decoration and was also hugely popular after the restoration of the monarchy in 1660. One reason for its continued use as a much-loved sampler motif I am sure is the fact that it has such a wonderful variety of styles and shapes and is thus a wonderful 'filler' for the end of a line or that awkward yawning gap where nothing else will seem to fit. Crowns and coronets were often worked with a letter beneath, indicating duke, earl and so on. This was for the purpose of 'marking' household linen in noble households. The initials stood for – king, duke, marquis, earl, viscount, lord, count and baron.

Mary Elizabeth Nicholson
1892

Mary Elizabeth Nicholson Sampler

DMC			
317 dark grey	ecru	351 deep apricot	730 dark sage
415 light grey	301 deep orange	842 flesh	733 light sage
922 pale orange	3772 dark pink beige	501 dark blue green	642 grey beige
3371 very dark brown	745 light yellow	926 slate blue	407 pink beige
738 light beige	310 black	902 maroon	223 deep pink
	951 very pale pink	347 red	

Mary Elizabeth Nicholson Sampler

DMC

Symbol	DMC colour
∩∩	317 dark grey
==	415 light grey
−−	922 pale orange
TT	3371 very dark brown
22	738 light beige
//	ecru
44	301 deep orange
55	3772 dark pink beige
77	745 light yellow
■■	310 black
◸◸	951 very pale pink
∷∷	351 deep apricot
↖↖	842 flesh
	501 dark blue green
∧∧	926 slate blue
▲▲	902 maroon
◻◻	347 red
−−	730 dark sage
//	733 light sage
++	642 grey beige
⊠⊠	407 pink beige
↑↑	223 deep pink

ABCDEFGHIJKL
MNOPQRSTUV
WXYZ 12345
Hannah Richards 1886
Not land but
learning
makes a man
complete
There is a path
that leads to truth.
Kitty
Fisher

ADDITIONAL PROJECTS

⁂ *The tiny Crown Miniature takes its crown motif and initials from the Mary Elizabeth Nicholson Sampler (chart, page 32–35). It is worked in cross stitch with two strands of black stranded cotton (floss) and gold thread, over one thread of white 28 count evenweave linen, within a decorative gold frame.*

⁂ *The design for the Birds in a Bush Card is taken from the Hannah Richards Sampler (chart, page 28–29), using the same 28 count cream evenweave linen and threads and mounted into a fold-over card (see page 141). Work in cross stitch, using two strands of stranded cotton (floss) over two threads of linen.*

⁂ *This delightful smaller version of the Hannah Richards Sampler (page 26) is worked in cross stitch, using two strands of stranded cotton (floss) over one block of 18 count Rustico fabric. To personalise the sampler, work out your name and the date in pencil on graph paper using the additional alphabets and numerals on page 135, and position as on the chart overleaf.*

⁂ *The tiny verse sampler (chart overleaf), 'Not Land But Learning', has been worked on specially dyed fabric (see page 10). Use two strands of black stranded cotton (floss) over one thread of cream 25 count Dublin linen.*

⁂ *This charming little sampler, 'There is a Path That Leads to Truth', uses elements from the larger Margaret Simcock Sampler (chart, page 24–25), and would be a delightful addition to a young girl's bedroom. A change of border gives a lighter feel to the design (see chart page 39), and the two girls each holding a rose replace the manor house as the central feature. The linen for this sampler (a cream 28 count evenweave), was dyed with Dylon's Koala Brown following the manufacturer's instructions. Work in cross stitch, using two strands of stranded cotton (floss) over two threads of linen, and one strand over one thread for the verse.*

⁂ *An enchanting Tie-on Pocket reminds us that at certain periods in history, this is how pockets were worn, and thus how Lucy Lockett was able to lose hers! The design features various motifs from this chapter – see instructions and chart on page 40–41.*

⁂ *The Miniature Band Sampler is worked on 4in (10cm) wide natural linen band using two strands of stranded cotton over two threads. I have taken some of the borders and an alphabet from the Band Sampler (chart, page 18–21) and put them together to form a totally different design. This is an idea you might like to try, either as an addition, or as an alternative to the larger design.*

⁂ *A miniature Shepherdess Picture derived from the Mary Elizabeth Nicholson Sampler (chart, page 32–35), uses two strands of stranded cotton (floss) over one thread of cream 32 count Belfast linen.*

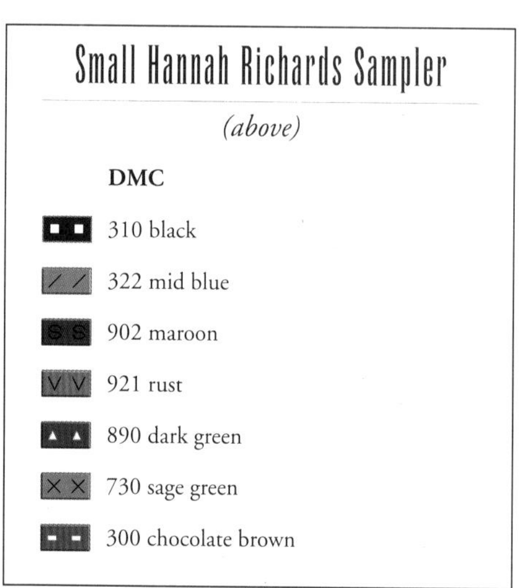

Small Hannah Richards Sampler

(above)

DMC

- 310 black
- 322 mid blue
- 902 maroon
- 921 rust
- 890 dark green
- 730 sage green
- 300 chocolate brown

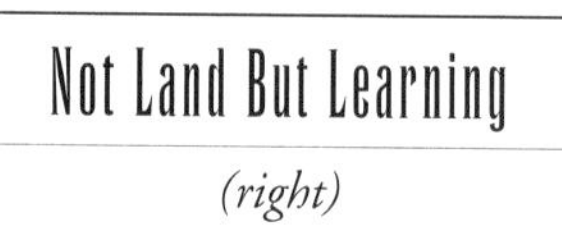

Not Land But Learning

(right)

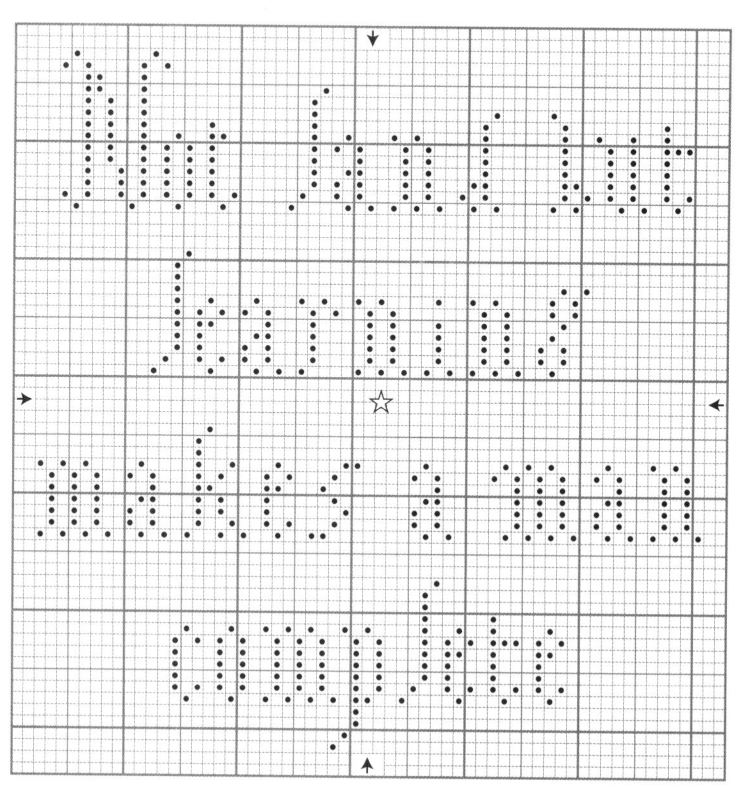

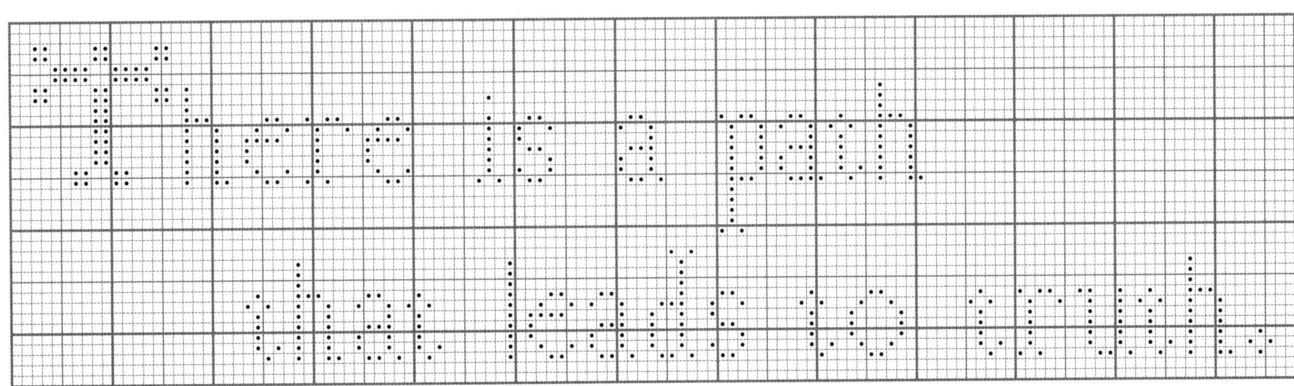

There is a Path That Leads to Truth

DMC		
3772 mid brown	223 deep pink	310 black
842 flesh	407 pink beige	Text – 310 black use 1 strand over 1 thread
927 slate blue	ecru	
	3053 mid green	

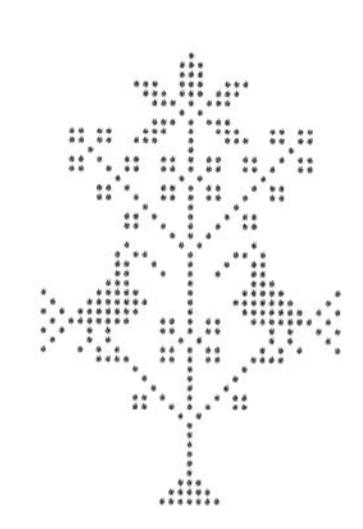

Tie-on Pocket

This enchanting tie-on pocket reminds us that at certain periods in history, this is how pockets were worn and thus how Lucy Lockett was able to lose hers!

Design size: 7½ x 6in (19 x 15cm)
Pocket size: 10in (25.5cm) wide x 9in (23cm) high
Stitch count: 106 x 88

* Two pieces 11 x 11in (28 x 28cm) cream Quaker cloth, 28 threads per inch (2.5cm) (or use a different fabric for backing)
* Stranded cottons (floss) as shown in the key
* One pack white bias binding
* White sewing cotton
* Tailor's chalk
* Small piece of white ribbon (optional)
* Use two strands of stranded cotton (floss) over two threads of linen.

1 Find the centre of the design and work outwards in cross stitch from this point following the chart.

2 If you wish to personalise the pocket, work out your name in pencil on graph paper using the upper case alphabet from the Hannah Richards Sampler (page 28) and the lower case from the House and Barn Sampler (page 76), or any of the additional alphabets shown on page 135.

3 When the embroidery is complete, mark a central vertical line with a row of tacking (basting) stitches. Trace the shape of the pocket from the template given onto a piece of folded paper matching the vertical line of the template with the fold line in the paper. Cut out your template. Match the fold to the vertical line of tacking (basting), and then mark the shape of the pocket on the fabric with tailor's chalk and cut out. Cut another piece of linen to match.

4 Tack (baste) the two pieces of linen wrong sides together, and machine or hand stitch a seam ¼in (0.5cm) in from the edge. Remove the tacking (basting) stitches, and sew the bias binding around the outer edge. Cut a vertical line as shown for the pocket entrance, and finish with bias binding. Fold the remaining binding in half lengthways and match the fold to the mid point of the pocket front. Attach the binding to the top of the pocket, sewing the extended overhanging lengths together to form ties.

5 Make a small bow from white ribbon and attach to the base of the pocket opening as shown.

To use this tie-on pocket template, follow the instructions in step 3.

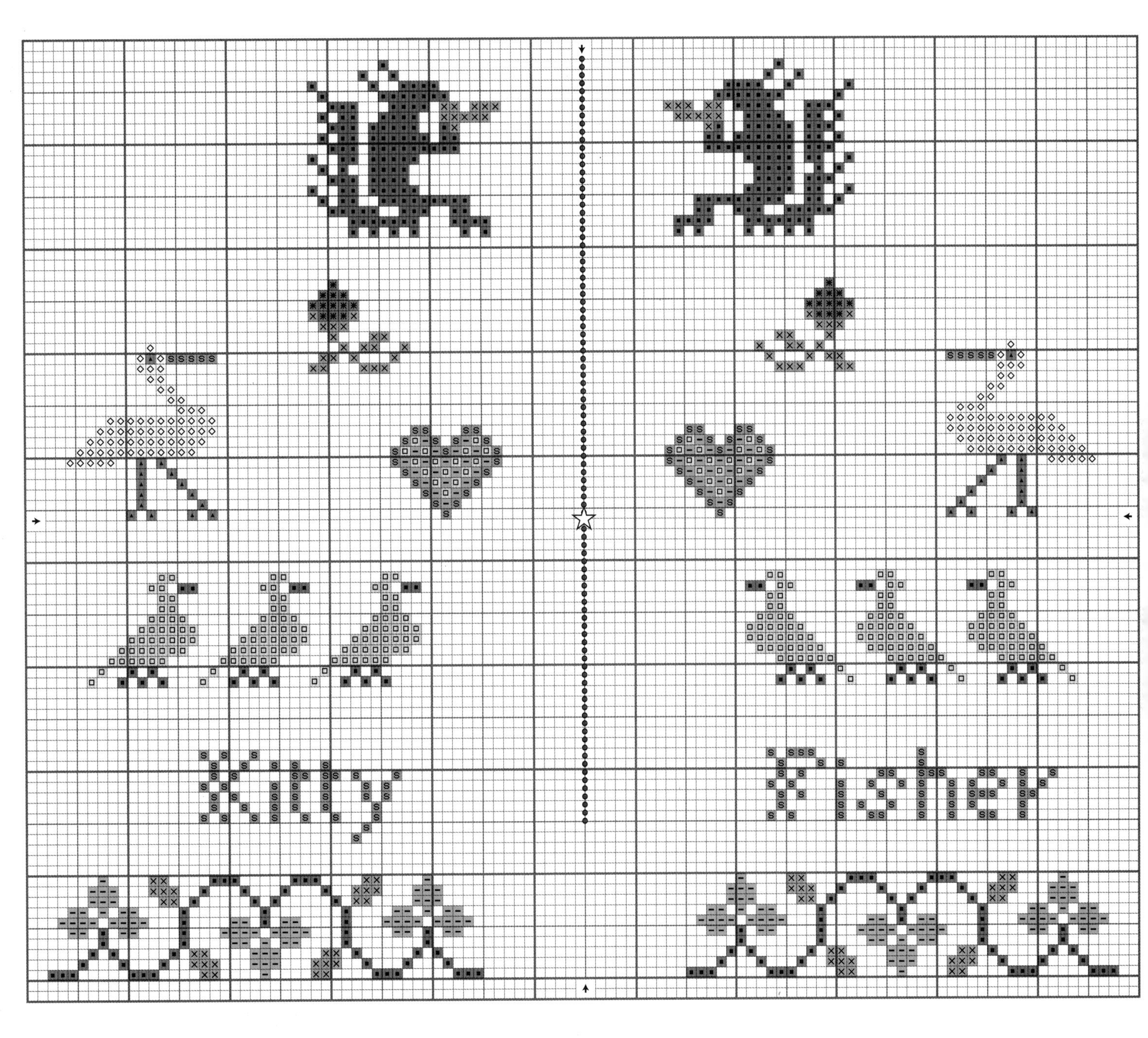

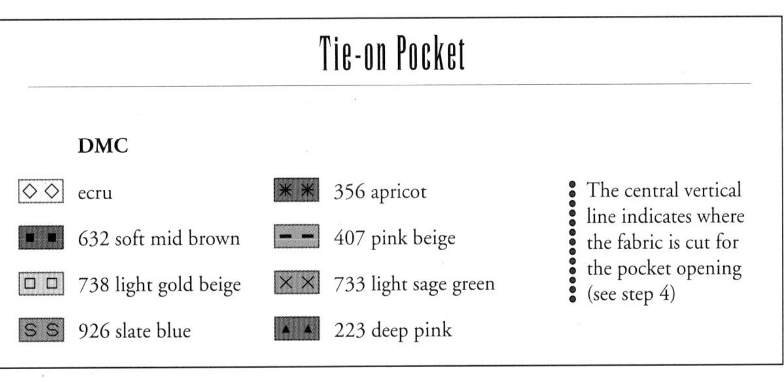
Tie-on Pocket

DMC

- ecru
- 632 soft mid brown
- 738 light gold beige
- 926 slate blue
- 356 apricot
- 407 pink beige
- 733 light sage green
- 223 deep pink

The central vertical line indicates where the fabric is cut for the pocket opening (see step 4)

MULTIPLICATION TABLE
1 2 3 4 5 6 7 8 9 10 11 12
2 4 6 8 10 12 14 16 18 20 22 24
3 6 9 12 15 18 21 24 27 30 33 36
4 8 12 16 20 24 28 32 36 40 44 48
5 10 15 20 25 30 35 40 45 50 55 60
6 12 18 24 30 36 42 48 54 60 66 72
7 14 21 28 35 42 49 56 63 70 77 84
8 16 24 32 40 48 56 64 72 80 88 96
9 18 27 36 45 54 63 72 81 90 99 108
10 20 30 40 50 60 70 80 90 100 110 120
11 22 33 44 55 66 77 88 99 110 121 132
12 24 36 48 60 72 84 96 108 120 132 144
Sarah Jennings
Train up a child
in the way he should go
and when he is old
he will not depart from it
Susanna Meeks
made in the 12th year
of her age 1858
ABCDEFGHIJK
LMNOPQRSTU
VWXYZ
abcdefghijklmno
pqrstuvwxyz
Hester Biddleton is my
name And with my
needle I wrought the
same. 1853
H B

SCHOOLROOM SAMPLERS

The social upheaval that began in the eighteenth century and continued throughout the nineteenth brought about the then revolutionary idea that girls should receive some form of formal education. Needlework had always been an important part of the educational regime but in the nineteenth century it came to the fore. Boarding schools for the middle classes, charity schools founded to provide elementary education for the children of the poor, and private or 'Dame' schools as they came to be known, all had one thing in common – the teaching of elementary embroidery by the working of a sampler. Although many and varied, these samplers can be broadly divided into two groups – decorative and utilitarian. Decorative samplers were mainly pictorial with an alphabet and pretty border, usually worked by children of the middle classes to show some competency in the art of needlework. These would be framed and displayed in the Victorian parlour by proud parents.

Utilitarian samplers, worked by the children of the poor (sometimes as young as five) were quite a different story. Good examples of this type of work are the Bristol Orphanage samplers. Utilitarian samplers often included a wide variety of alphabets, borders and coronets, and were worked in one shade only. This type of sampler would have been presented as proof to a prospective employer of a young girl's ability to mark household linen in a life of domestic service. In large houses all linen was marked with the owner's initials and in noble families with the appropriate crown or coronet. The style of both sets of samplers depended on many things – the competency, artistry and wit of the teacher, and the willingness and capability of the pupil to either obey very strict guidelines or, through a genuine love of the subject, to somehow introduce an element of originality into the work. It is fascinating to study old samplers and try to imagine which category the embroiderer fell into.

The Polly Kirkwood Sampler

'This I did so you may see
What care my parents took of me.'

This sampler, worked in cross stitch and backstitch contains one of the most popular verses seen on samplers of this period. Children were encouraged by their teachers and the church to honour their parents. This design, not a true reproduction as such, was inspired by similar works of the period. Although children of poorer families were still producing utilitarian samplers to prepare them for a life in service marking household linen, most of the samplers which have survived are decorative enough to show that they were intended not only as a practice piece but for display.

Design size: 12¼ x 10½ in (31 x 26.5cm)
Stitch count: 185 x 221

- 17 x 15in (43 x 38cm) 18 count Rustico fabric
- Stranded cottons (floss) as shown in the key
- Use two strands of stranded cotton (floss) over one block of fabric.

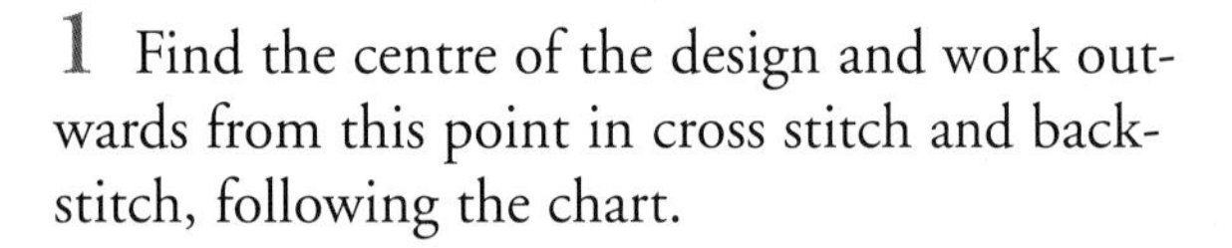

1 Find the centre of the design and work outwards from this point in cross stitch and backstitch, following the chart.

2 If you wish to personalise the sampler by substituting your own name, age and so on, work out your details in pencil on graph paper (additional alphabets and numerals can be found on page 135), and position as shown on the chart. If your name is too long to fit the space, simply omit two of the trees.

3 Stretch, mount and frame as required (see advice on pages 137–139).

Samplers as Birth Certificates

At the beginning of the First World War, women were called upon to work in factories and in industry to take the place of their menfolk. Birth certificates as we know them were not commonplace, and in certain cases where women had to prove their age, they would take along their schoolroom sampler as proof of their date of birth.

This I did so you
What care my parents
1821

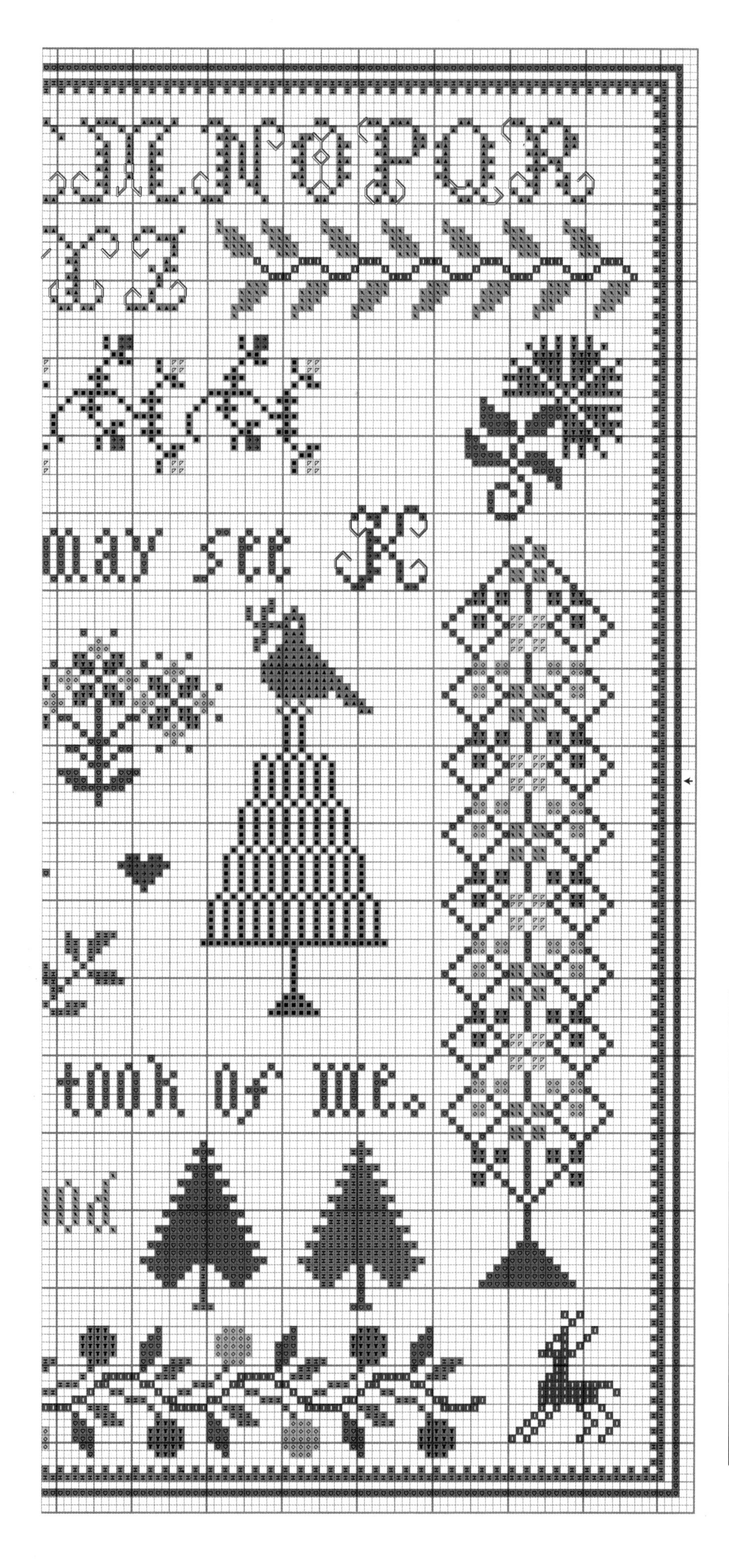

Polly Kirkwood Sampler

DMC

- 3787 mid brown
- 3021 dark brown
- 3772 dark pink brown
- 930 dark blue
- 502 blue green
- 3325 light blue
- 356 apricot
- 730 dark sage green
- 372 mid green grey
- 758 mid pink

The Hester Biddleton Sampler

A multitude of motifs typical of the period – birds, trees, dogs, crowns and plants – are included in this charming sampler. The words '. . . *is my name and with my needle I wrought the same*', is commonly found on samplers. This type of sampler was frequently the product of a 'Dame' school, and although the overall look of the sampler was often dictated by the teacher, children were allowed to personalise their samplers and use their imagination, within certain guidelines.

This one is full of childish fun, and, with the exception of the crowns (a favourite addition to samplers of all eras), is filled with things that Hester would have seen every day.

DESIGN SIZE: 13½ x 7¼IN (34 x 18.5CM)
STITCH COUNT: 235 x 131

❋ 18 x 11in (46 x 28cm) 18 count Rustico fabric

❋ Stranded cottons (floss) as shown in the key

❋ Use two strands of stranded cotton (floss) over one block of fabric.

1 Find the centre of the design and following the chart work outwards from this point in cross stitch (with the exception of the dog's tail which is worked in backstitch).

2 If you wish to personalise the sampler by substituting your own name and the date, work out your details in pencil on graph paper, using any of the additional alphabets on page 135 that will fit the space, and then position as shown on the chart.

3 Stretch, mount and frame as required (see advice on pages 137–139).

SAMPLER VERSES

If a verse was to be included in a sampler, the expected subject matter would commonly have been religious, moralistic, or even concerning death. We find it very strange in this day and age that young minds could concern themselves with such serious thoughts, but in an age of high infant mortality, the following verse, written by a child of seven, would not have raised an eyelid.

And now my soul another year
Of thy short life is past
I cannot long continue here
And this may be my last.

ABCDEFGHIJK
LMNOPQRSTU
VWXYZ
abcdefghijklmno
pqrstuvwxyz
Hester Biddleton is my
name And with my
needle I wrought the
same. 1853
H
B
ONE HUNDRED
POEMS
FOR CHILDREN

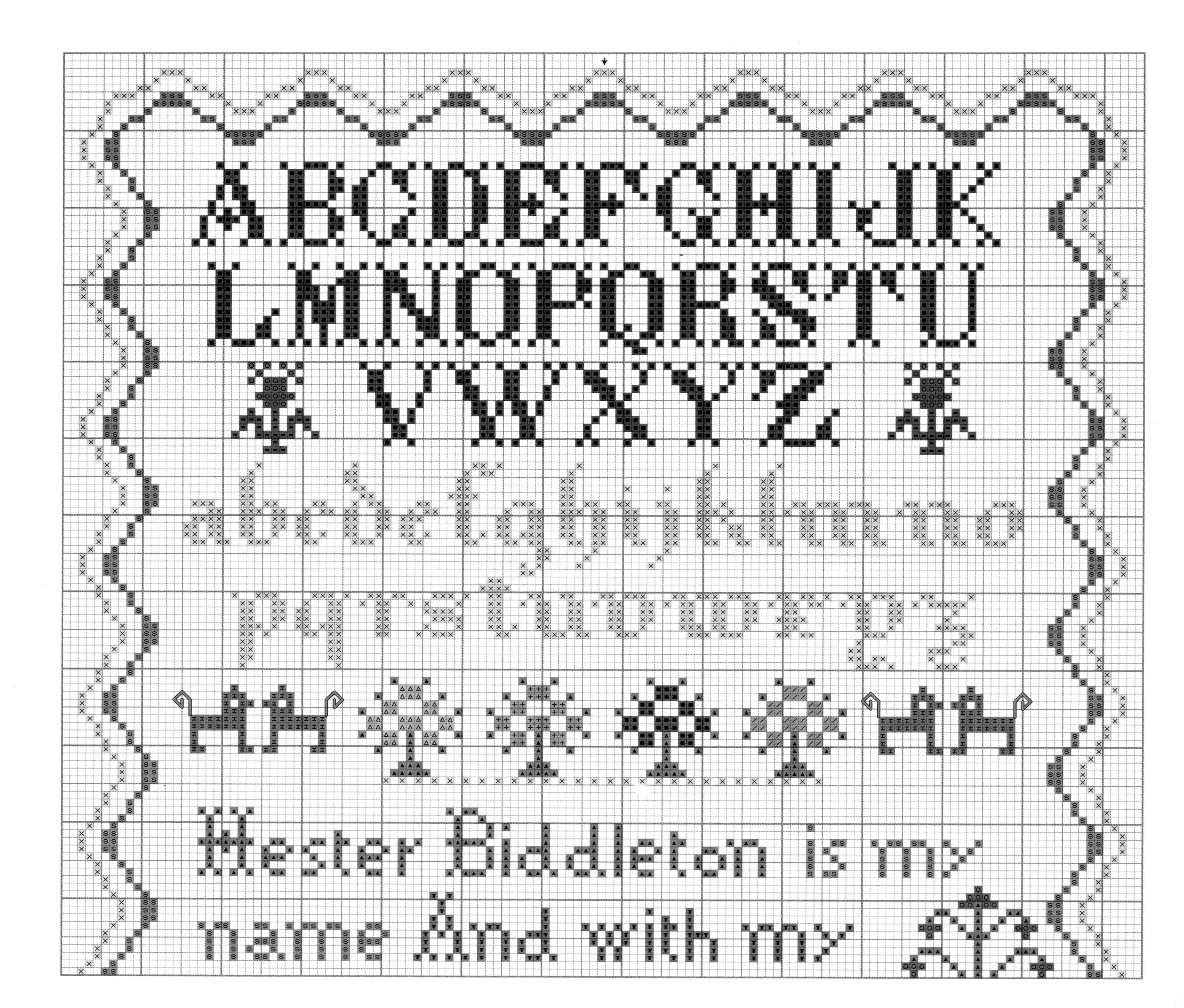
ABCDEFGHIJK
LMNOPQRSTU
VWXYZ
abcdefghijklmno
pqrstuvwxyz
Hester Biddleton is my
name And with my

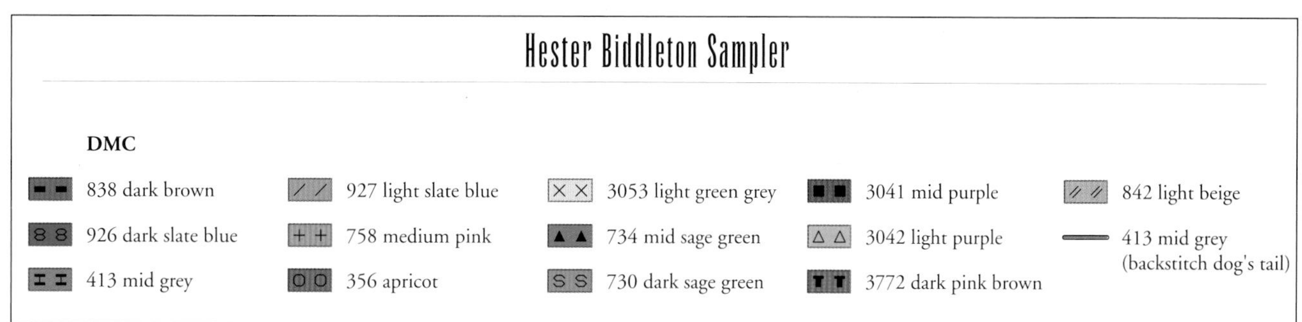
Hester Biddleton Sampler
DMC
838 dark brown
926 dark slate blue
413 mid grey
927 light slate blue
758 medium pink
356 apricot
3053 light green grey
734 mid sage green
730 dark sage green
3041 mid purple
3042 light purple
3772 dark pink brown
842 light beige
413 mid grey (backstitch dog's tail)

The Susanna Meeks Sampler

This particular sampler is not a reproduction of an original, but is rather made in the style of the time and given a date to correspond. In the mid-nineteenth century the teaching of needlework was considered to be of paramount importance and all schools would have included it in their curriculum. Children were encouraged to use moral and 'improving' verses.

DESIGN SIZE: 7 x 8IN (18 x 20CM)
STITCH COUNT: 99 x 112

❊ 11 x 12in (28 x 30.5cm) sand Quaker cloth No. 322, 28 threads per inch (2.5cm)

❊ Stranded cottons (floss) as shown in the key

❊ Use two strands of stranded cotton (floss) over two threads of linen, except for the verse and name/age details which are worked with one strand over one thread. To work the lettering use cross stitch and follow the charts on this page and page 54. The first letter of each row is also charted on the main chart on page 54 to help you position the words correctly.

1 Find the centre of the design and work outwards in cross stitch from this point following the chart.

2 If you wish to substitute a name, age or so on, work out your details in pencil on graph paper and then position on the main chart as shown.

3 Stretch, mount and frame as required (see pages 137–139 for advice).

Each dot represents a cross stitch using 1 strand of stranded cotton (floss) over 1 thread of linen, with colour changes as follows:
Name – 355 rust
Numerals and year – 740 orange
Verse and remaining words – 730 sage green

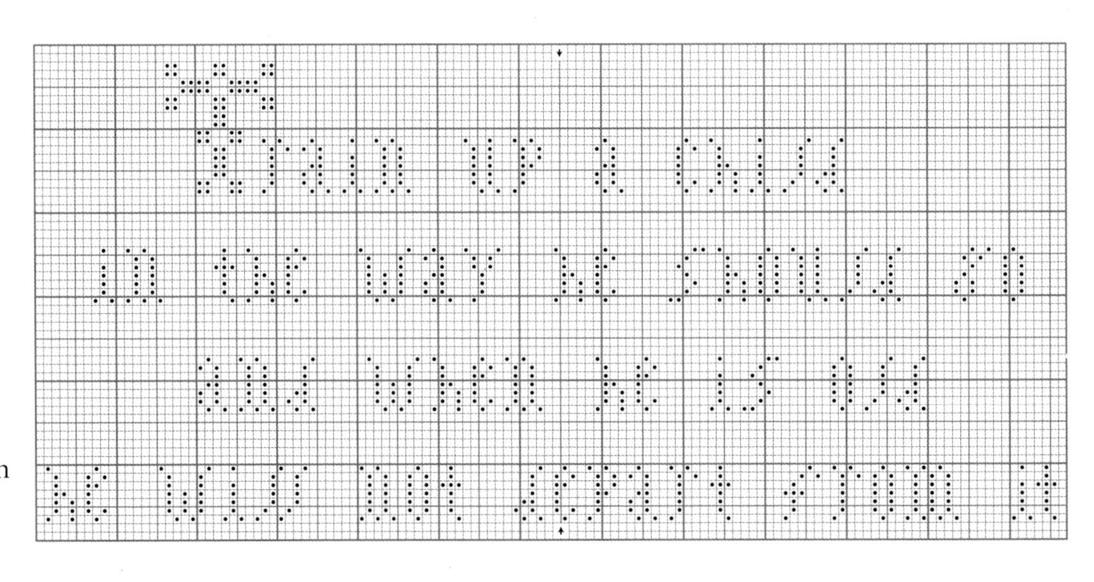

Train up a child
in the way he should go
and when he is old
he will not depart from it
Susanna Meeks
made in the 12th year
of her age 1858
S'ENFILENT FACILEMENT
PIQUEFORT
IMPORTÉ D'ALLEMAGNE
LUSTRE

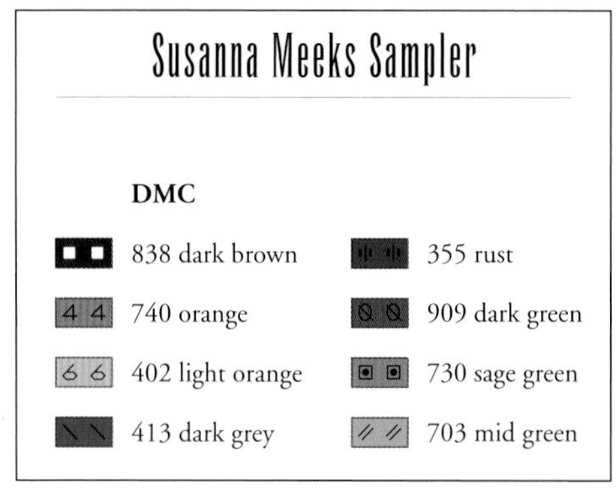
Susanna Meeks Sampler
DMC
838 dark brown
740 orange
402 light orange
413 dark grey
355 rust
909 dark green
730 sage green
703 mid green

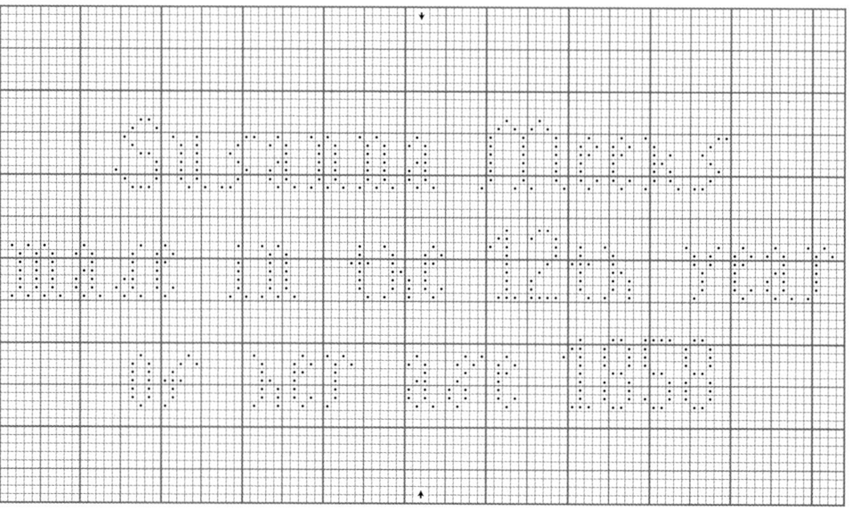

Sarah Jennings' Multiplication Table

Surviving examples of this type of utilitarian sampler are often found to have their roots in Scotland. The Edinburgh Museum of Childhood has a similar example to this one. This type of sampler can be placed under the heading 'teaching samplers' and although they must have tested the skill of the embroiderer in some small way, they were primarily a teaching tool.
I have kept this design simple, without much in the way of ornamentation or colour (most were made using just one shade), for authenticity and to reflect the original purpose. If you wish you could add colour and further details – a border for example.

Design size: 14 x 10½in (35 x 27cm)
Stitch count: 205 x 157

❋ 18 x 15in (46 x 38cm) natural evenweave linen, 28 threads per inch (2.5cm)

❋ DMC stranded cotton (floss) 310 black

❋ Use two strands of stranded cotton (floss) over two threads of linen.

1 Find the centre of the design and work outwards in cross stitch from this point following the chart.

2 If you wish to substitute a name, work out your details in pencil on graph paper and then position on the main chart as shown.

3 Stretch, mount and frame as required (see pages 137–139 for advice).

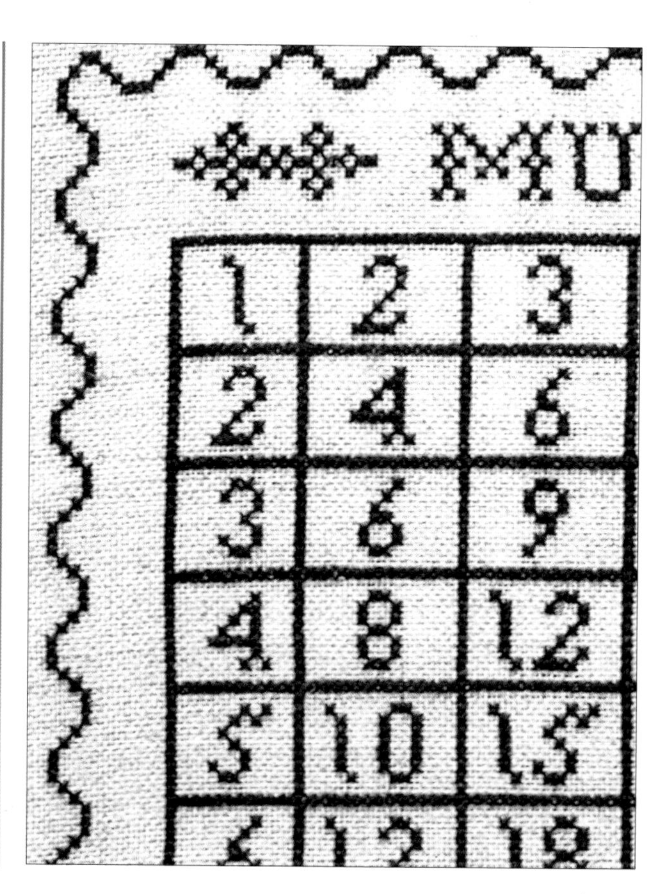

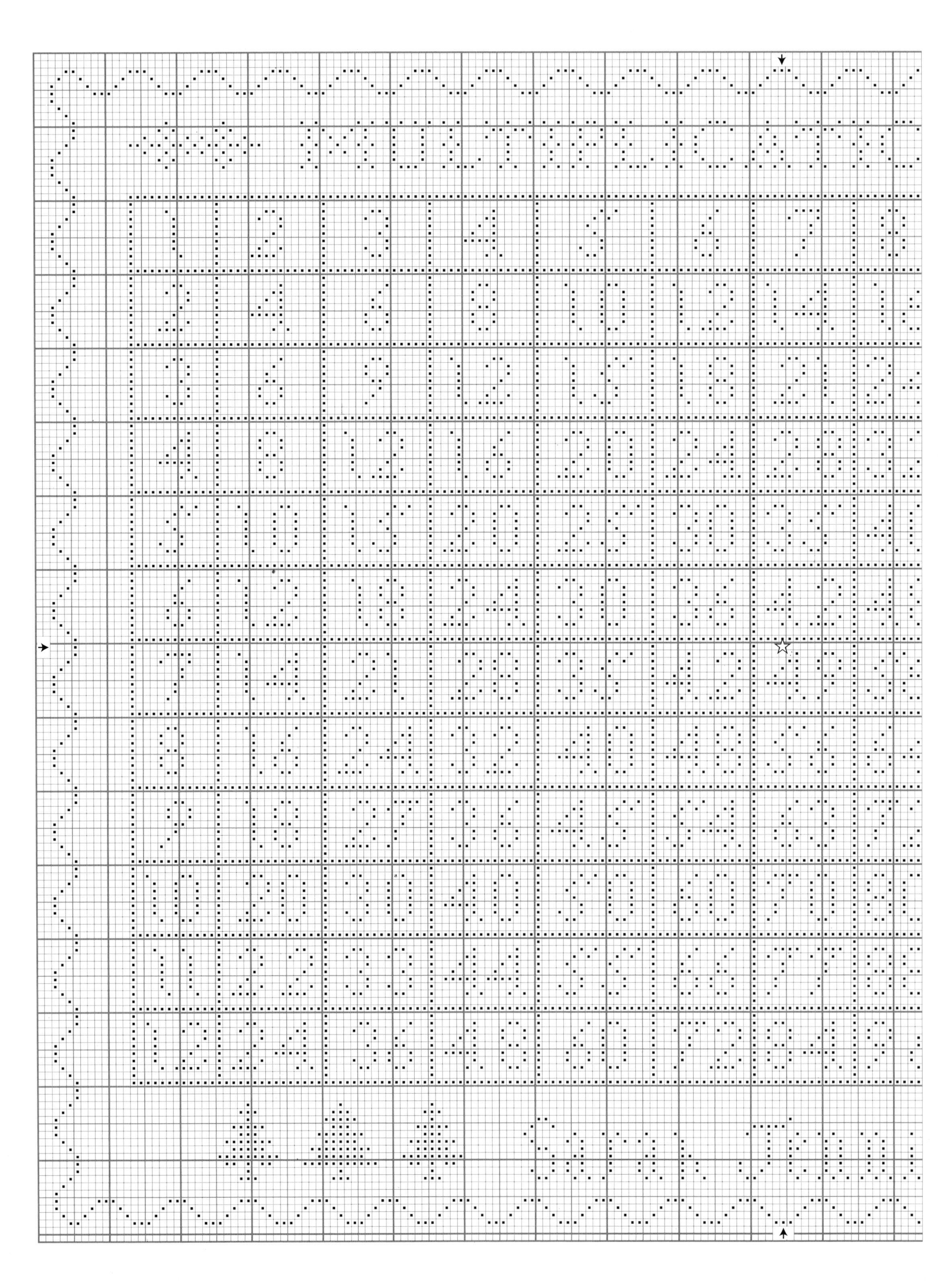

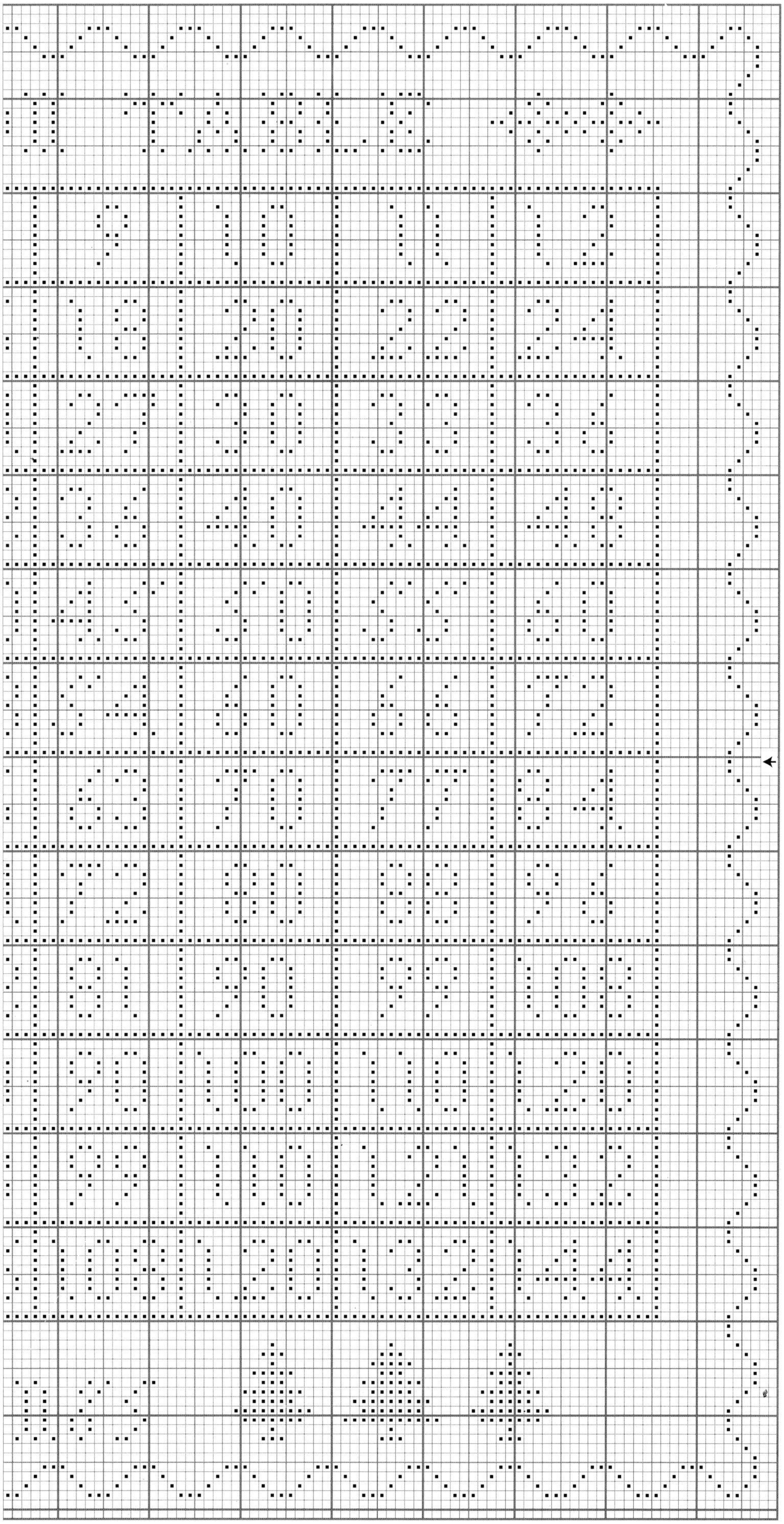

Sarah Jennings' Multiplication Table

DMC

▪ ▪ 310 black

Polly Kirkwood
1821
1853
HB
ABCDEFGHIJK
LMNOPQRSTU
VWXYZ
The Mystery of Carach Dhu

ADDITIONAL PROJECTS

❊ *The design for the cushion is taken from the Hester Biddleton Sampler (page 48). It is worked in tent stitch (see Stitch Library page 12) with DMC Laine Colbert tapestry wool over one thread of 10 count single thread white canvas, 15in (38cm) square. See chart on page 60 and instructions for Making Up a Cushion on page 142.)*

❊ *The pincushion design is taken from the Susanna Meeks Sampler (page 52). It is worked in tent stitch (see Stitch Library page 12) with DMC Laine Colbert tapestry wool over one thread of 10 count single thread white canvas, 8in (20cm) square. See chart on page 63 and instructions for Making Up a Pincushion on page 142.)*

❊ *The Miniature Hester Biddleton Sampler shows just how easy it is to take elements from a design (page 48) and transform them into a totally different project. It is worked in cross stitch with one strand of 310 black stranded cotton (floss) over one thread of 32 count Belfast linen (see chart, page 61).*

❊ *Three smaller projects have been adapted from the Polly Kirkwood Sampler. The Facing Birds Picture (chart page 63) is worked in cross stitch over two threads of 28 count cream linen with Caron Watercolours thread 'Teak' No. JF113927. The Small Polly Kirkwood Sampler (chart page 62) is worked in cross stitch in the same shades as the larger version on page 44 but on 32 count cream Belfast linen. The bookmark (chart page 46) is worked in cross stitch on a 4in (10cm) wide linen band with Caron Watercolours 'Fiesta' No. LCO10817.*

❊ *A pencil case personalised with a child's name would make a useful gift for a child starting school. This one (chart page 63) was worked in cross stitch with two strands of 310 black stranded cotton (floss) over one block of 18 count Rustico fabric.*

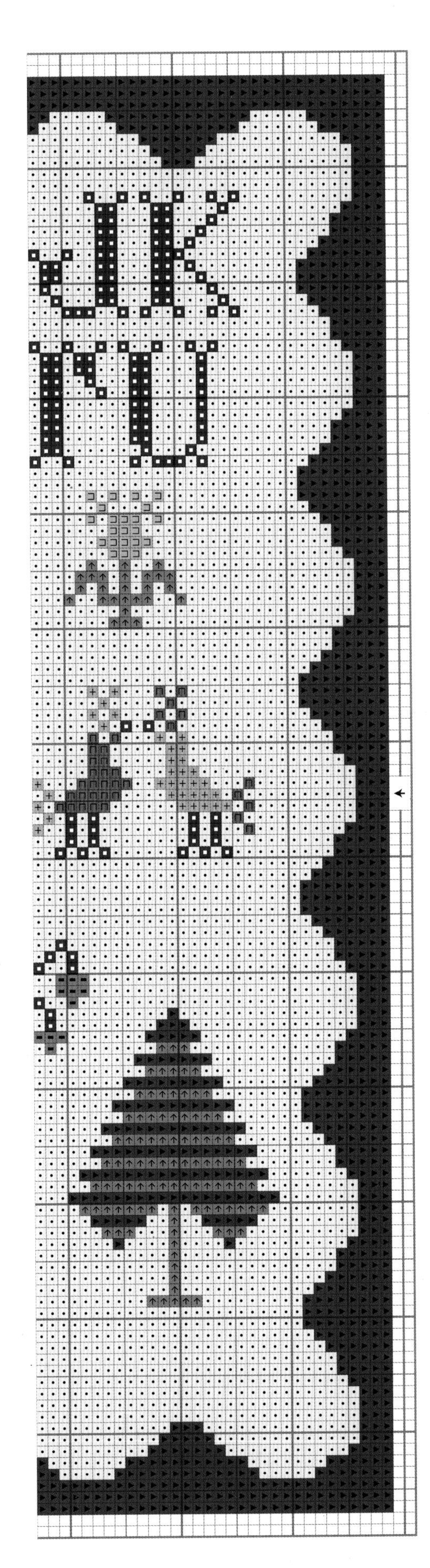

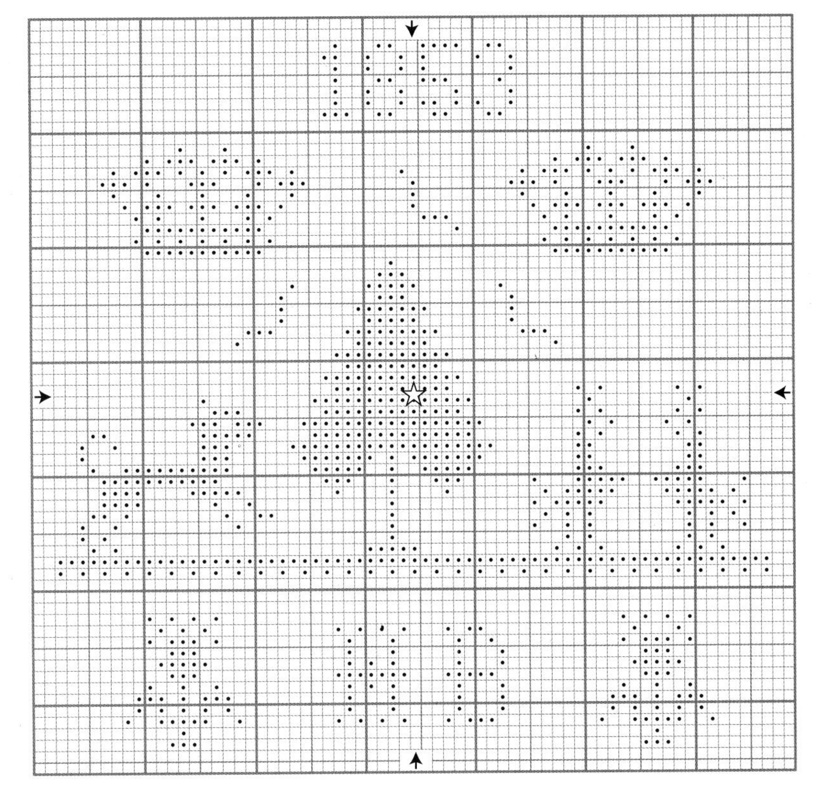

Miniature Hester Biddleton Sampler

DMC

• •	310 black

Cushion

DMC Laine Colbert

• •	7500 cream
▪ ▪	7535 very dark brown
S S	7463 light beige
▬ ▬	7690 dark slate grey
+ +	7692 light slate grey
► ►	7890 very dark green
↑ ↑	7573 sage green
/ /	7457 mid brown
▲ ▲	7459 light chocolate brown
⊐ ⊐	7951 strawberry pink
⊓ ⊓	7226 light plum

Small Polly Kirkwood Sampler

(above)

DMC

Symbol	Colour	Symbol	Colour
I I	3371 dark brown	⊥ ⊥	760 light pink
И И	926 slate blue	♡ ♡	730 dark sage green
+ +	356 apricot	I I	3829 golden brown

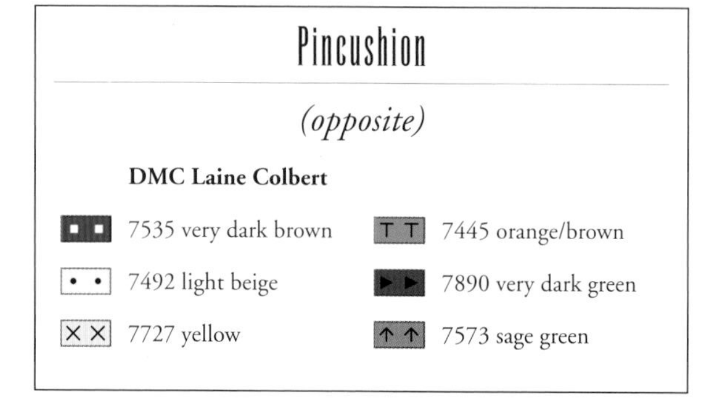

Pincushion

(opposite)

DMC Laine Colbert

Symbol	Colour	Symbol	Colour
▫ ▫	7535 very dark brown	T T	7445 orange/brown
• •	7492 light beige	▶ ▶	7890 very dark green
X X	7727 yellow	↑ ↑	7573 sage green

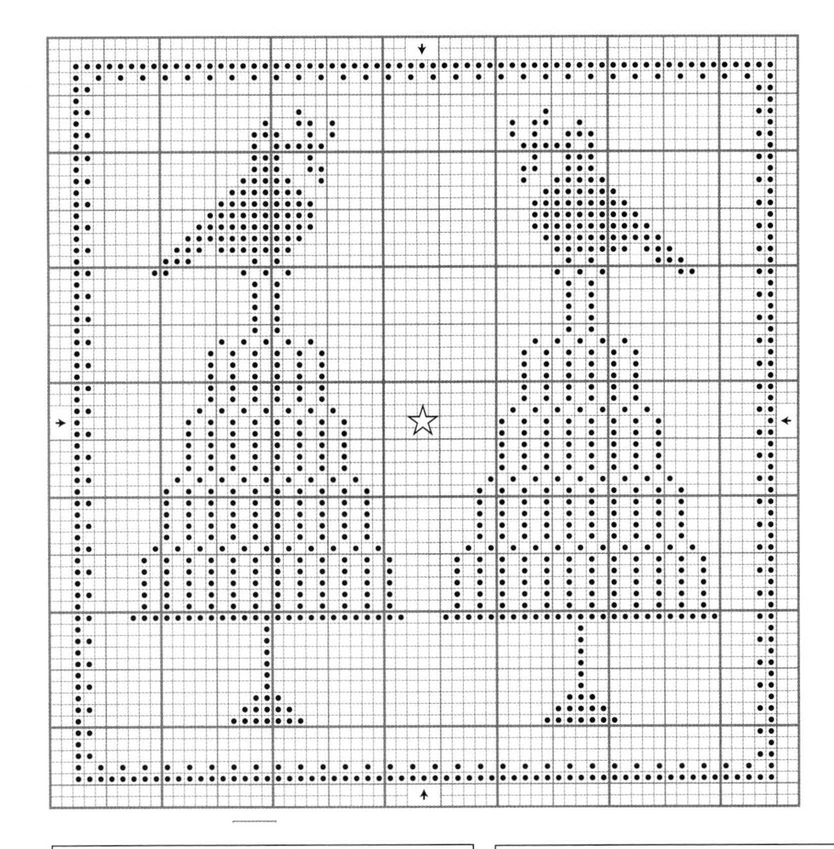

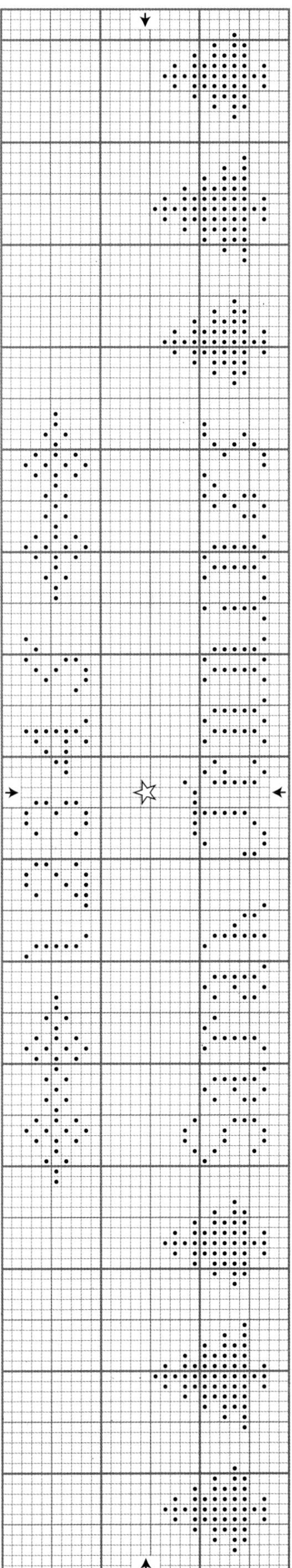

Facing Birds Picture *(above)*

Pencil Case *(right)*

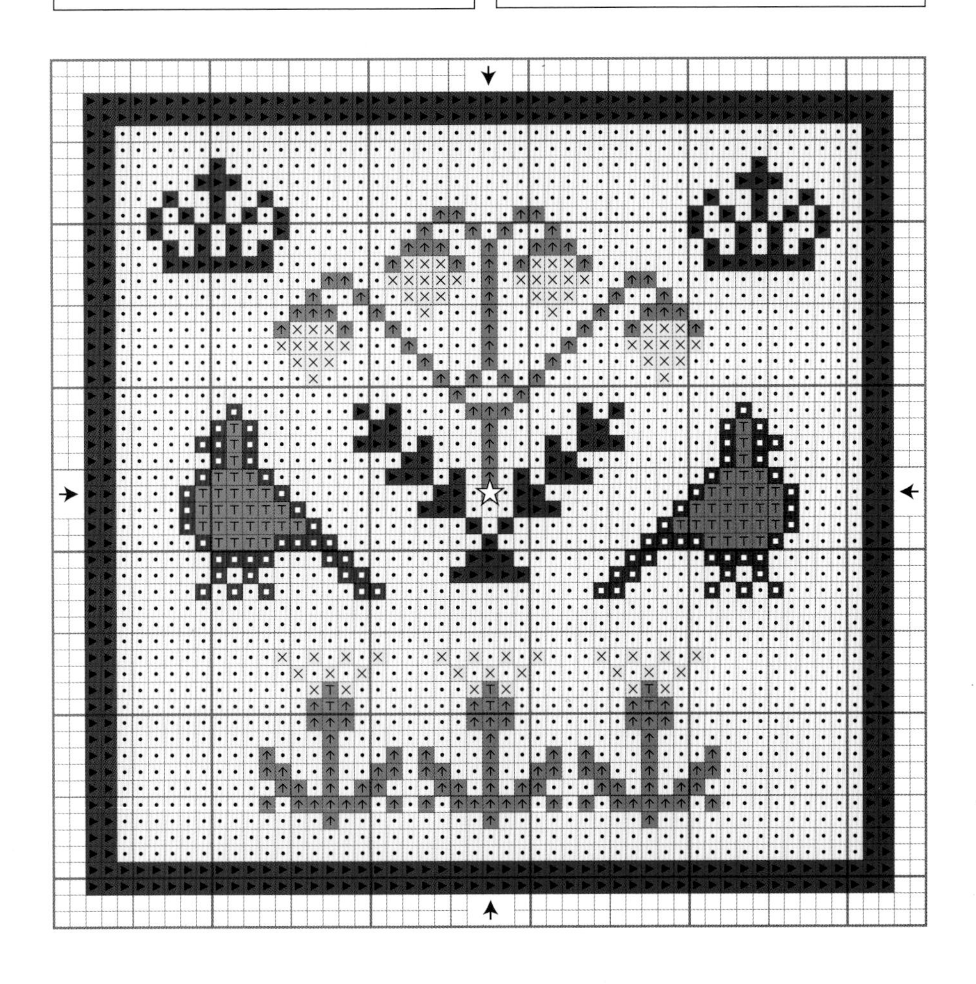

To celebrate the
25th
Wedding Anniversary
of Chris + Brenda Keyes
1st April 1997
To celebrate the
Engagement
of
Sarah & Mark
15th Apr 1998
Elizabeth & Andrew
15th August 1998
When two fond hearts
in love unite
The Yoke is easy
the burden light.
To celebrate the
50th
Wedding Anniversary
of Irene & James Keyes
21st Aug 1993

CELEBRATION SAMPLERS

Strangely, the last five centuries have produced thousands of samplers commemorating the death of a loved one, but very few celebrating life's joyous events (the most notable being the Jane Bostocke sampler of 1598).

The Victorians in particular took mourning very seriously indeed. They followed the example set by Queen Victoria, whose beloved husband Albert died at a relatively early age. From that tragic day, the queen wore only black, and unconsciously condemned not only the court but the entire country to an era of mourning and solemnity. Entire catalogues of mourning clothes were available. Paintings, statues, and especially samplers were affected by the prince's untimely death. Weeping willows, urns, catafalques, and even elaborate tombs were frequently embroidered on commemorative samplers of the period. Infant mortality was high, and many samplers featured the name or names of brothers and sisters who had died. Gloomy verses warning of impending death were rife and sadly, children as young as the age of five were embroidering their samplers with verses such as:

And now my soul another year of thy short life is past
I cannot long continue here and this may be my last.

I am extremely happy to say that this tradition of gloom and despondency has died a death. Happily, we now use our time and skill to embroider works that bring pleasure and delight. Wedding, engagement, anniversary, and new home samplers are very widely worked, and very popular indeed. Although of course it is fitting to honour the departed, it is certainly a change for the better that our generation is now far more likely to commemorate life's celebrations in their samplers.

Engagement Sampler

Betrothal samplers as such do not seem to have been made in the past. Indeed marriage samplers, although more common, are still somewhat rare. Today, we see an engagement as a celebration of intent rather than a binding contract. This sampler could certainly be described as a joyful celebration of intent, with its pretty border dancing around the floral motifs and text. It is also infinitely adaptable. Simply change the word engagement to marriage, anniversary, or retirement. Or adapt the text to commemorate a special birthday. This book features lots of alphabets in varying styles and sizes, so if you wish to alter or add to the text, simply substitute another.

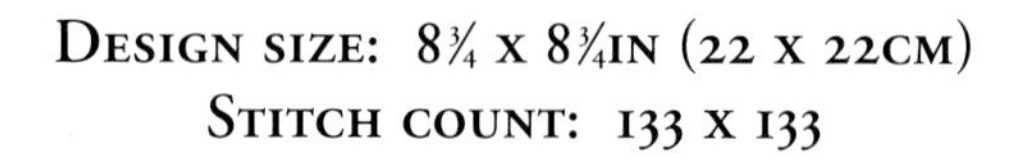

DESIGN SIZE: 8¾ x 8¾IN (22 x 22CM)
STITCH COUNT: 133 x 133

❊ 13 x 13in (33 x 33cm) cream Belfast linen, 32 threads per inch (2.5cm)

❊ Stranded cotton (floss) as shown in the key

❊ Use two strands of stranded cotton (floss) over two threads of linen throughout.

1 Find the centre of the design and work outwards in cross stitch from this point following the chart.

2 To personalise the sampler, work out names, dates etc using the alphabets and numerals given on the additional alphabets page 135, in pencil on graph paper and position as shown on the chart.

3 Stretch, mount and frame as required (see pages 137–139 for advice).

BREACH OF PROMISE

Until 1970, when the law was changed, anyone who became engaged to marry entered into a contract that could be legally binding. An engagement or betrothal was taken so seriously that if one partner broke off the engagement without the agreement of the other, they could be sued for breach of promise.

In some societies, betrothal is still an important part of the marriage process, with the giving of a ring, earrings or other item of jewellery marking the obligation.

To celebrate the
Engagement
of
Sarah & Mark
15th Apr
1998

To celebrate
of
Sarah &
15th Apr
19

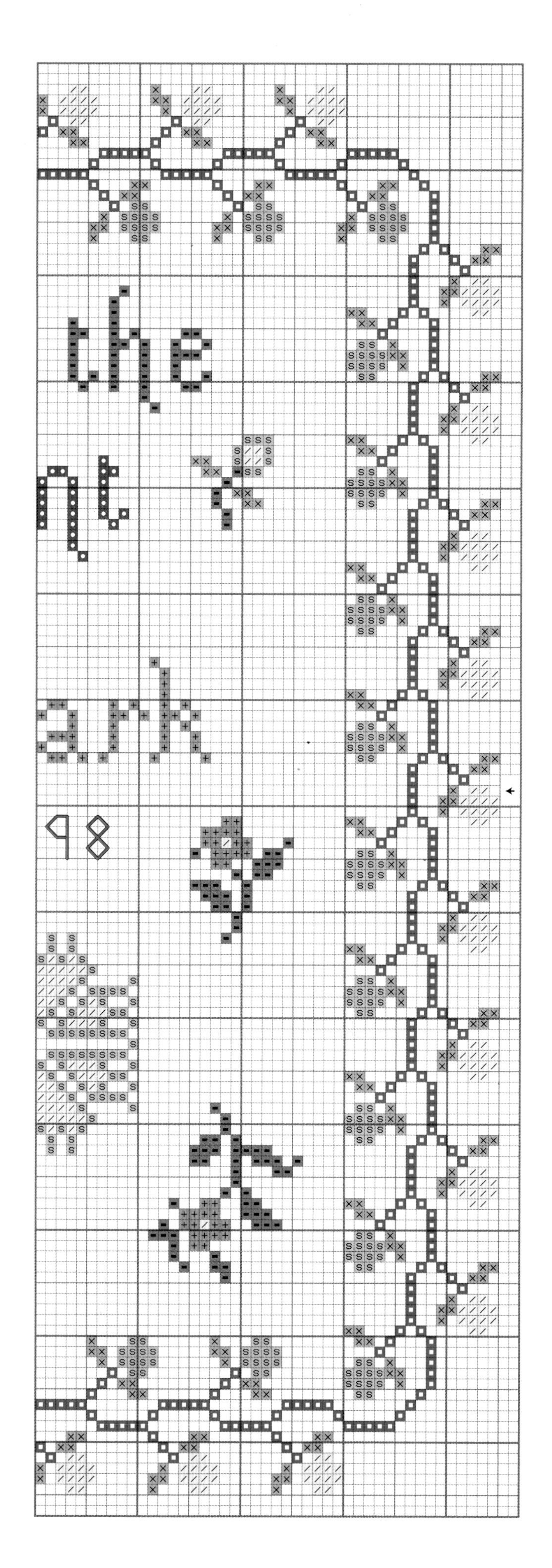

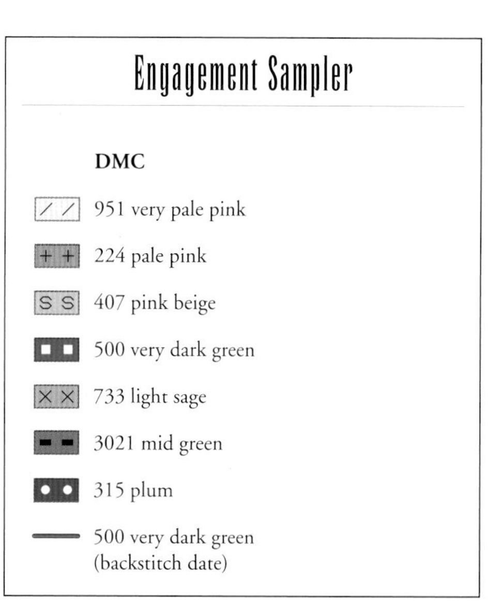

Altered Age

If you study old samplers, you will come across examples, particularly those from the late eighteenth and early nineteenth centuries, where the age of the stitcher has been unpicked and either left blank, or obviously changed. Until I became engrossed in the work of Jane Austen, I was convinced that the stitcher herself had unpicked this obvious giveaway to her age, but given that most samplers were framed and displayed at the time for all to see, I now feel sure that many a 'Mrs Bennett' will have felt the urge to aid her unmarried daughter's chances of finding a beau!

Wedding Ring Sampler

This delicate wedding sampler has the unusual addition of two gold-coloured rings suspended from a ribbon garland held by two cherubs. This delightful design would make a treasured gift for a newly wedded couple.

The central floral motif has been isolated from a well loved and much used larger floral border which has featured on many samplers over the centuries. It is fascinating to study samplers and see the same or similar motifs and borders on work not only from many countries but also across the centuries.

DESIGN SIZE: 4¾ x 5IN (12 x 13CM)
STITCH COUNT: 129 x 141

✻ 8 x 9in (20.5 x 23cm) cream evenweave linen, 28 threads per inch (2.5cm)

✻ Stranded cottons (floss) as shown in the key

✻ Two 'wedding rings' (from Framecraft, see Suppliers page 143)

✻ Use one strand of stranded cotton (floss) over one thread of linen throughout.

1 Find the centre of the design and work outwards in cross stitch from this point following the chart on page 72. If you find it a great strain on your eyes to work over just one thread, simply work in cross stitch with two strands of cotton (floss) over two threads of the linen. Remember though to allow sufficient extra fabric as this will double the size of the design – see page 8 for advice.

2 To personalise the sampler, work out names, dates, initials and so on in pencil on graph paper (using the alphabet given or additional ones on page 135), and then position as shown on the chart.

3 Attach the two rings by oversewing in position as shown on the chart, using two strands of DMC stranded cotton (floss) 223 deep pink.

4 Stretch, mount and frame as required (see pages 137–139 for advice).

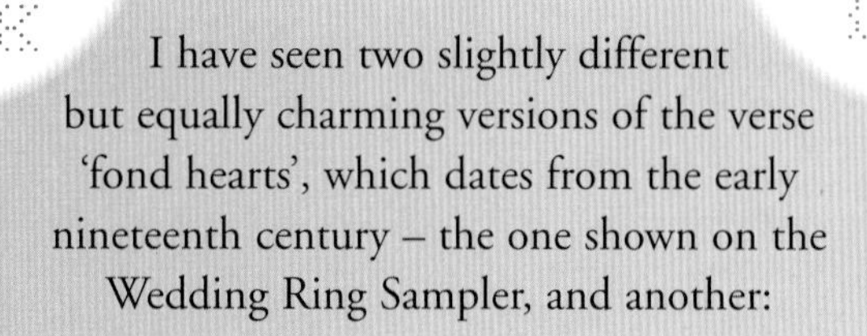

I have seen two slightly different but equally charming versions of the verse 'fond hearts', which dates from the early nineteenth century – the one shown on the Wedding Ring Sampler, and another:

When two fond hearts as one unite,
The yoke is easy and the burden light.

Elizabeth & Andrew
15th August 1998
E
A
When two fond hearts
in love unite
The yoke is easy
the burden light.

Elizabeth & And
13th August
E
When two fond he
in love unite
The Yoke is eas
the burden ligh

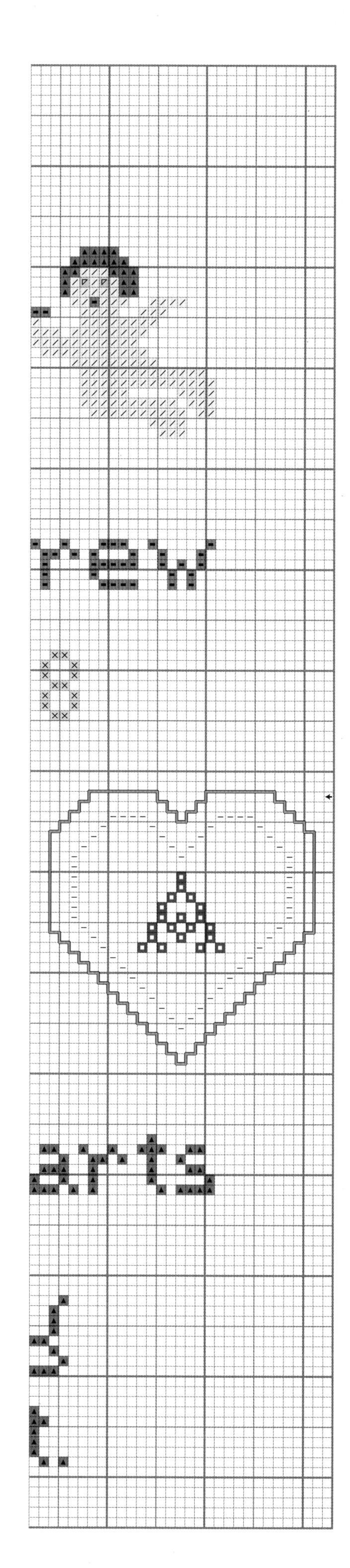

Wedding Ring Sampler

DMC	
ecru	223 warm pink
632 mid brown	3052 light green grey
3774 flesh	3051 dark green grey
3820 dull yellow (or substitute wedding rings)	3042 light lilac
927 light slate blue	Backstitch 224 light pink (heart outlines)

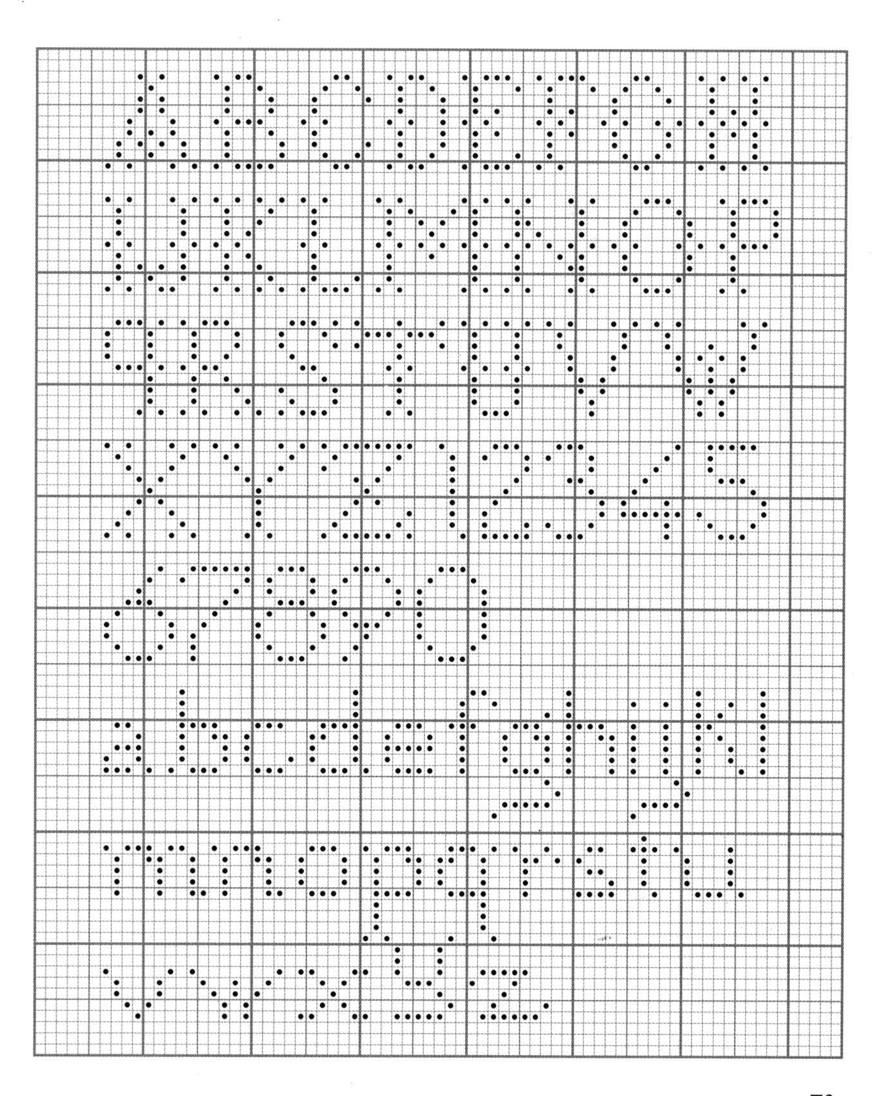

House and Barn Sampler

This sampler is loosely based on the early nineteenth century House and Barn Samplers of Portsmouth, New Hampshire. Each contained a house, barn, row of trees, fence and bird house. Verses varied but all contained two or three alphabets and baskets of flowers or fruit. What makes this particular style interesting is that it was taught at different schools by different tutors, the Misses Mary Ann Smith and Mary Walden*. Perhaps the similarities occurred because they were friends and shared ideas, or perhaps they attended the same school and the idea evolved from their tutor.

* *Betty Ring – Girlhood Embroidery*

DESIGN SIZE: 11¼ X 10½ IN (29 X 27CM)
STITCH COUNT: 159 X 145

❋ 15 x 14in (38 x 36cm) sand Quaker cloth No. 322, 28 threads per inch (2.5cm)

❋ Stranded cottons (floss) as shown in the key

❋ Use two strands of stranded cotton (floss) over two threads of linen except for the verse and name/age details (below) which are worked with one strand of 310 black over one thread of linen. For the name/age, follow the chart below. The first letter of each line is also charted on the main chart on page 76 to help you position the words correctly.

1 Find the centre of the design and work outwards in cross stitch following the chart.

2 If you wish to substitute a name, age etc, work out your details in pencil on graph paper, using the alphabets given here or from the additional alphabets on page 135, and then position as shown on the main chart.

3 Stretch, mount and frame as required (see page 137–139 for advice).

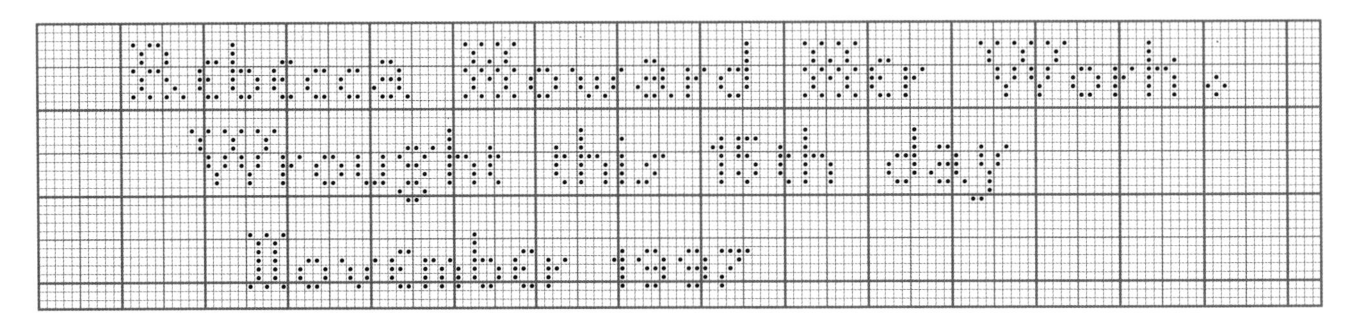

ABCDEFGHIJKLMNOPQRSTUV
WXYZ
abcdefghijklmnopqrstuvwxyz 123456
ABCDEFGHIJKLMNOPQRSTU
VWXYZ
Rebecca Howard Her Work.
Wrought this 15th day
November 1997
Church House Farm

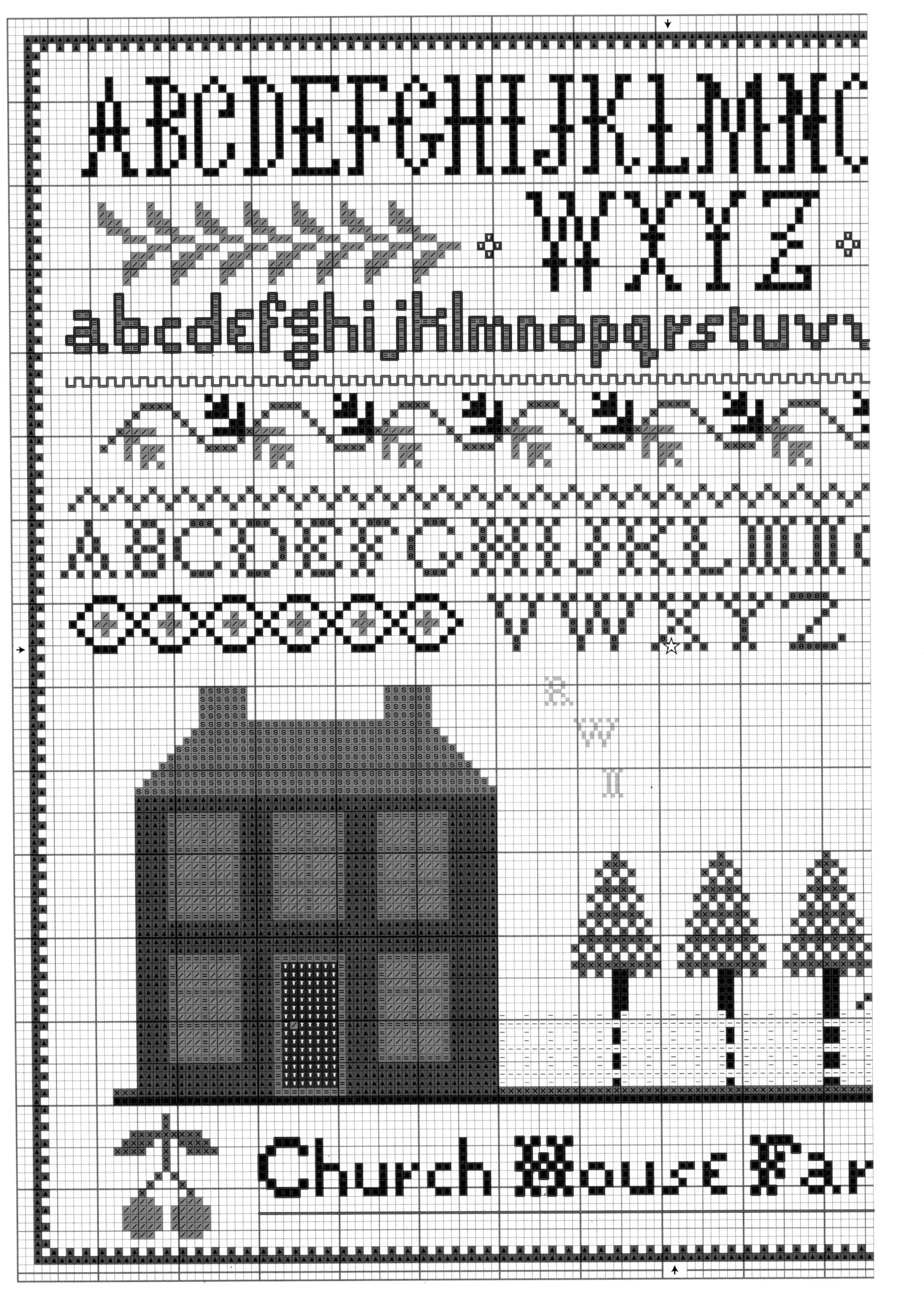

ABCDEFGHIJKLMN
WXYZ
abcdefghijklmnopqrstuv
ABCDEFGHIJKLMN
VWXYZ
R
W
I
Church House Far

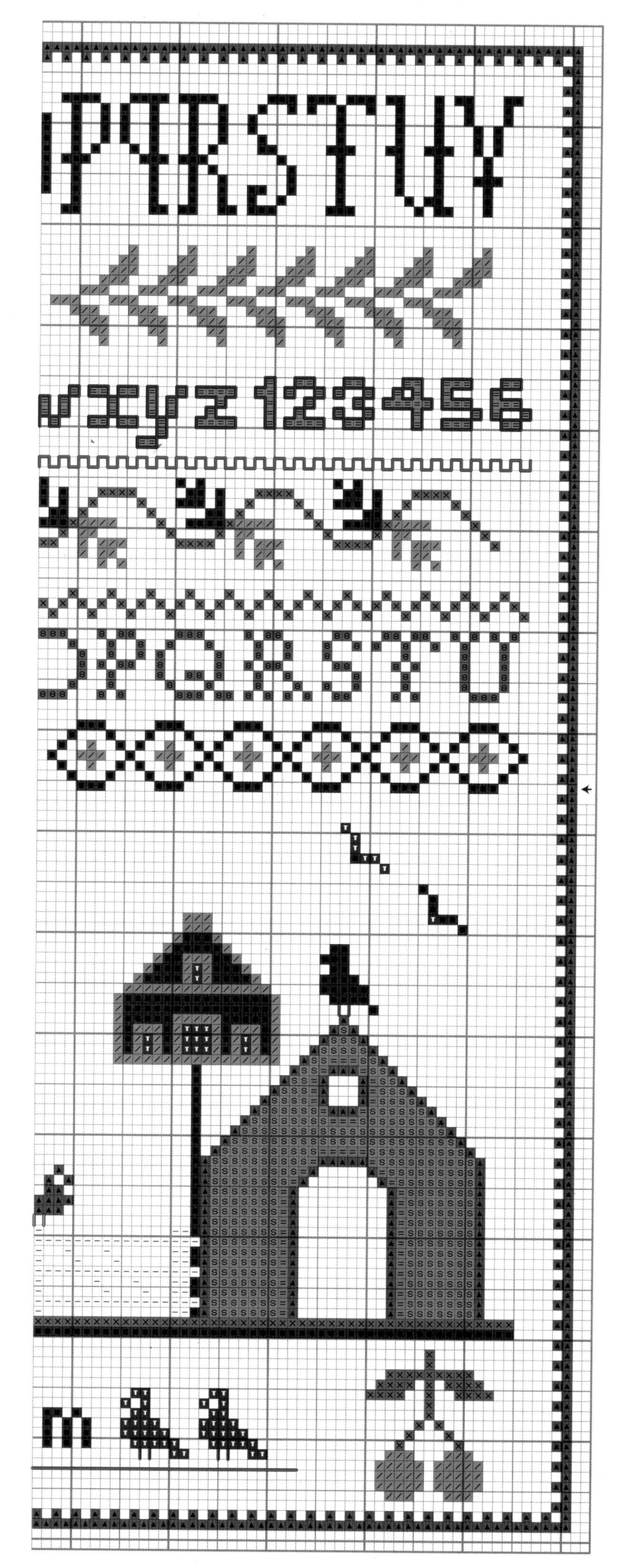

House and Barn Sampler

DMC

- S S 642 grey brown
- – – ecru
- ▲▲ 632 mid brown
- / / 680 gold
- T T 924 antique blue
- 8 8 501 green blue
- = = 926 slate blue
- ■■ 300 chocolate brown
- X X 730 sage green

Backstitch

- 501 green blue
- Outline lower case letters of alphabet and numerals with 2 strands 501
- Work the backstitch line under the house name with 2 strands 501
- Outline capital letters of house name with 1 strand 924 (optional)

Silver and Golden Wedding Anniversary Samplers

Elegant borders were chosen to commemorate two important occasions – Silver and Golden wedding anniversaries. Marlitt thread highlights certain stitches, and the numerals have been worked with either silver or gold thread. This is a very practical chart, as the same border can be used to commemorate other anniversaries. For a Ruby wedding anniversary for example, simply substitute ruby coloured thread in the border, and change the number of years.

DESIGN SIZE: 9¾ x 7½in (25 x 19cm)
STITCH COUNT: 139 x 99

* 14 x 12in (36 x 30.5cm) cream linen, 28 threads per inch (2.5cm)

* Stranded cottons (floss) as shown in the key

* Marlitt thread No. 1012

* DMC gold thread D282 or silver D281

* Use two strands of stranded cotton (floss) and one strand of Marlitt thread over two threads of linen for all cross stitches and backstitches. The tiny Algerian eyelet stitches in the inner border and the tent stitch used for the numerals are worked over one thread (see Stitch Library page 12).

1 For this design, it is best to start work at the top left-hand corner of the border. To do this, measure 3¼in (8cm) down and 3¼in (8cm) in from the side of your fabric and place the first stitch (the corner stitch of the right angle) here. Complete the outer and then the inner border.

2 Work out your details in pencil on graph paper using the backstitch alphabet and the numerals given, and then align as shown on the chart.

3 Stretch, mount and frame as required (see pages 137–139 for advice).

WEDDING ANNIVERSARIES

1 year	– Cotton	13 years	– Lace
2 years	– Paper	14 years	– Ivory
3 years	– Leather	15 years	– Crystal
4 years	– Fruit or Flowers	20 years	– China
5 years	– Wood	25 years	– Silver
6 years	– Iron or Sugar	30 years	– Pearl
7 years	– Wool	35 years	– Coral
8 years	– Bronze	40 years	– Ruby
9 years	– Copper or Pottery	45 years	– Sapphire
10 years	– Tin	50 years	– Gold
11 years	– Steel	55 years	– Emerald
12 years	– Silk or Fine linen	60 years	– Diamond
		70 years	– Platinum

To celebrate the
50th
Wedding Anniversary
of Irene & James Keyes
21st Aug 1993
To celebrate the
25th
Wedding Anniversary
of Chris + Brenda Keyes
1st April 1997

To celebrate the
25 th
Wedding Anniversa
of
0123456789

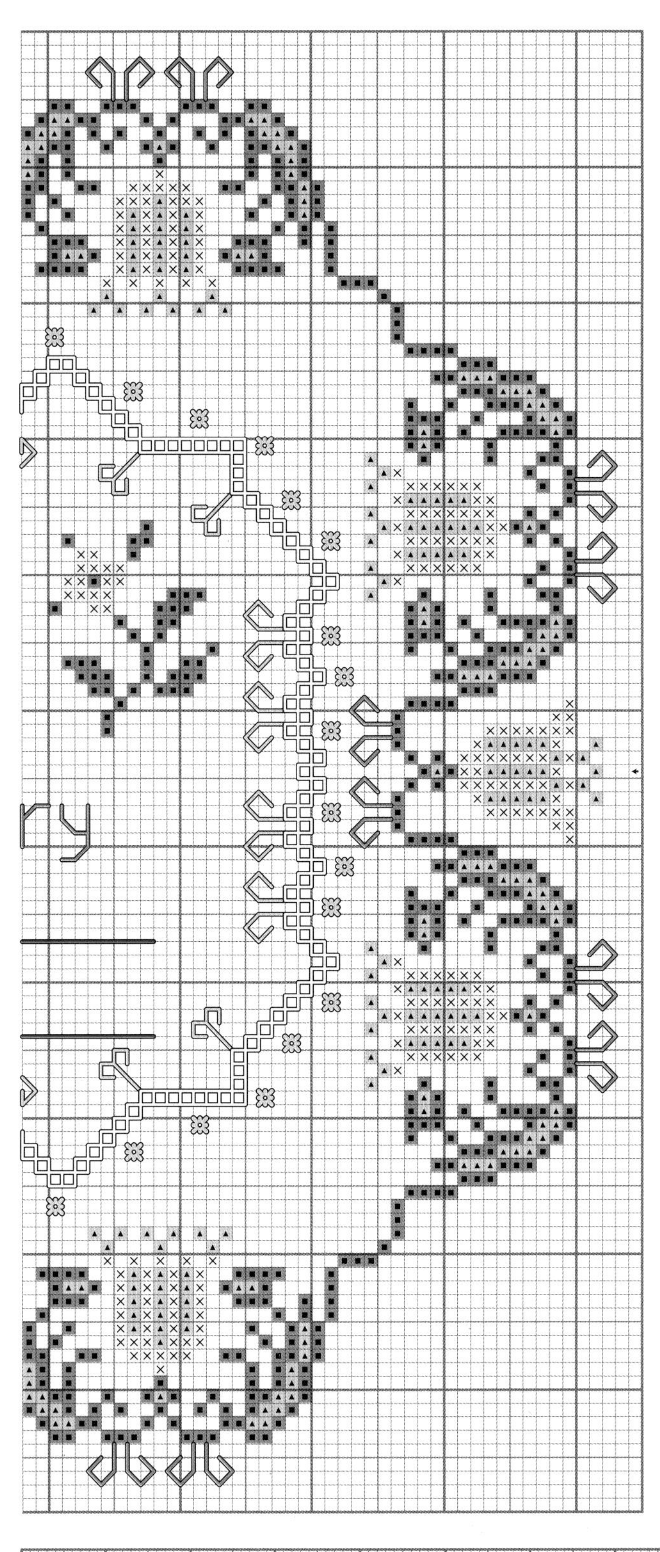

Silver or Golden Wedding Anniversary Sampler

Silver

- DMC stranded cotton (floss) ecru
- DMC stranded cotton (floss) 927 slate blue
- DMC silver D281
- Marlitt 1012 cream
- Marlitt 1012 cream (eyelets and finials)
- Text 927 slate blue (position on line)

Gold

- DMC stranded cotton (floss) ecru
- DMC stranded cotton (floss) 422 dull gold
- DMC gold D282
- Marlitt 1012 cream
- Marlitt 1012 cream (eyelets and finials)
- Text 422 dull gold (position on line)

ABCDEFGHIJKLMNOPQRSTUVWXYZ
abcdefghijklmnopqrstuvwxyz
1234567890

Welcome
Sarah & Mark
17
Elizabeth & Andrew
15th August 1998
E
A

ADDITIONAL PROJECTS

Life's celebrations are a time to show people that you care, and what better way to do so than to make a special gift to commemorate the occasion. If time is pressing and you cannot make one of the larger samplers in this chapter, why not make a card or small picture adapted from one of the charts.

* *The Engagement Card is adapted from the Engagement Sampler on page 66. It is a classic design worked in cross stitch with two strands of ecru stranded cotton (floss) over one thread of 28 count moss green linen (see chart overleaf). You could buy a ready-made card mount or make your own fold-over card (see page 141). As well as using this design for a card, it would look delightful as a small framed picture, with one or two toning mounts in cream and pale green.*

* *The pretty Wedding Ring Pillow (see instructions on page 85) uses the same chart as the Wedding Ring Sampler on page 70 but the verse has been omitted. If you wish you could embroider the two 'wedding rings' as well as adding real ones so that when they are removed at the ceremony the design will be complete. Elements from this design could also be used for a card.*

* *The Welcome Picture and Barn Card would make perfect gifts for a couple just setting up home. I deliberately did not add the words 'New Home', as the work would then inevitably become dated. Both cards use motifs from the House and Barn Sampler (chart, page 76) and are worked in cross stitch on sand 25 count Dublin linen, using two strands of stranded cotton (floss) over two threads of linen. See page 141 for making a fold-over card.*

* *The Silver and Golden Wedding Anniversary Samplers design (chart, page 80) can be adapted to suit many other occasions – silver or ruby wedding anniversaries for example. Here it has been adapted to a 50 Golden Years Card, that could equally well be used as a framed picture. Worked on white 16 count Aida, the card has gold thread worked over one block of fabric for the backstitching and cross stitching. See page 141 for making the design into a fold-over card. This particular design has fine gold cord glued around the edge of the aperture and an added gold tassel.*

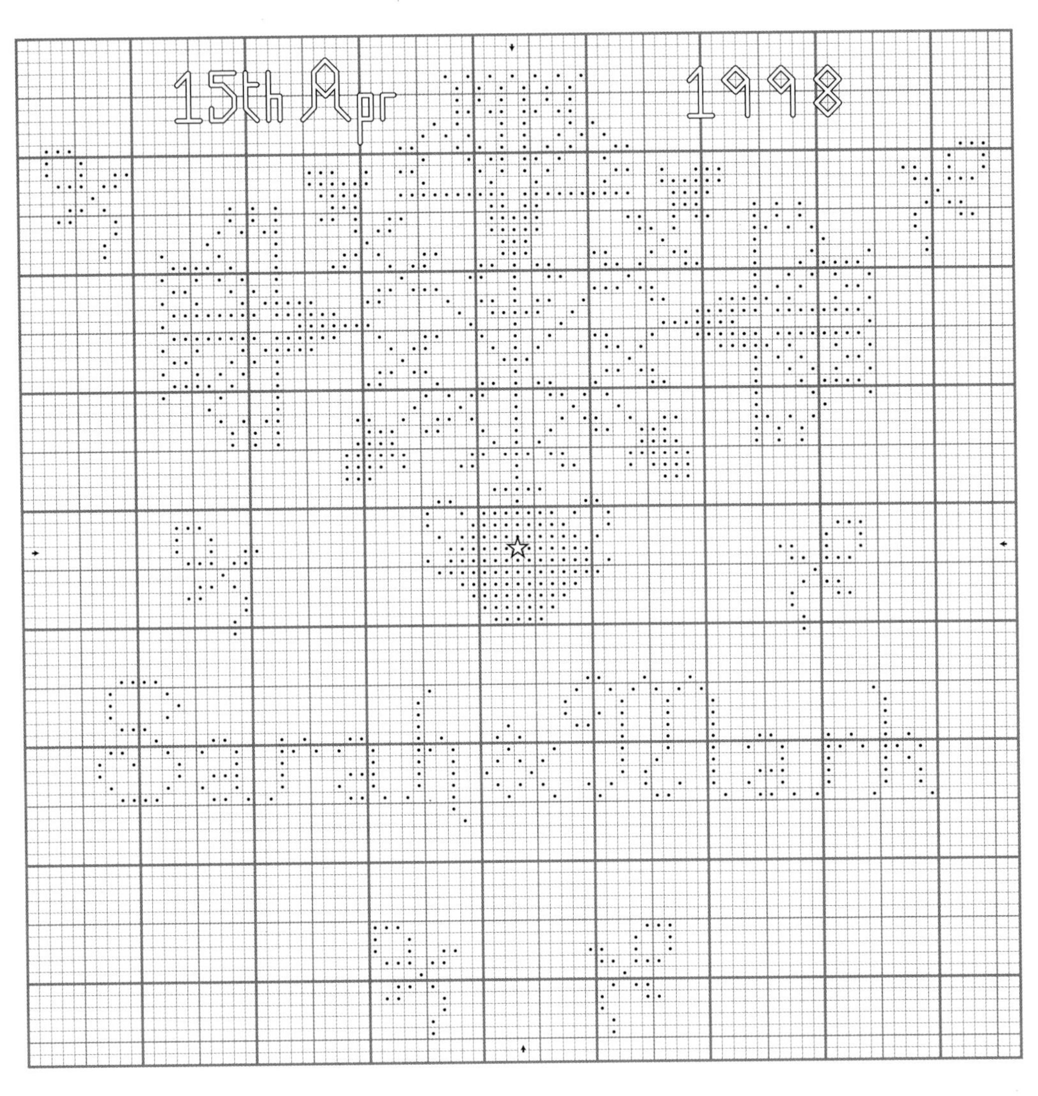

Engagement Card

(left)

DMC

• • ecru

Backstitch date – ecru

50 Golden Years Card

(below)

DMC

6 6 D282 gold

Backstitch D282 gold

Adam alone in Paradise did grieve
And thought Eden a desert without Eve,
Until God pitying his lonesome state
Crown'd all his wishes with a lovely mate.
Then why should men think mean,
or slight her,
That could not live in Paradise
without her.

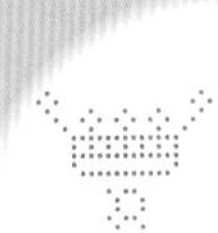

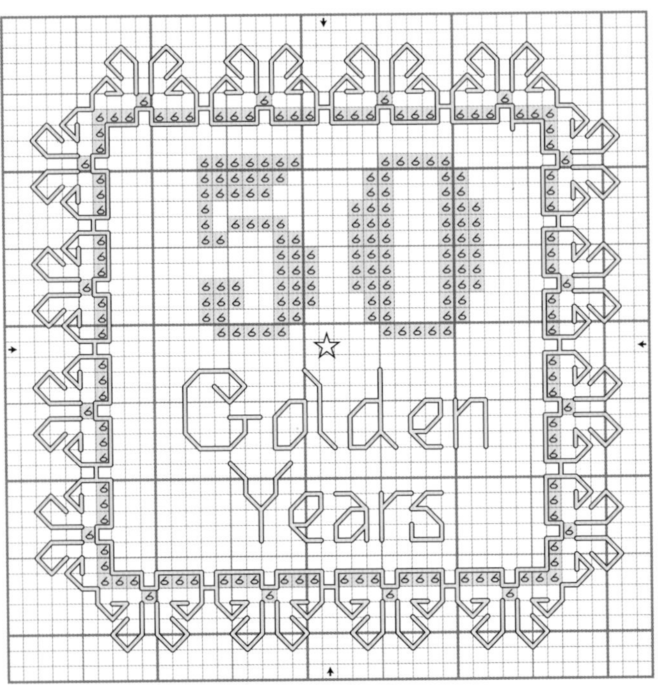

Wedding Ring Pillow

Ring pillows, like confetti and horseshoes, are fast becoming an established part of wedding tradition. This particular 'pillow', complete with ribbons, cherubs and flowers, is sure to add that special touch to the day.

Design size: 9¼ x 7in (23 x 18cm)
Stitch count: 129 x 96

❊ 13 x 11in (33 x 28cm) cream Quaker cloth, 28 threads per inch (2.5cm)

❊ Stranded cottons (floss) as shown in the key

❊ Two wedding rings (from Framecraft, see Suppliers page 143)

❊ Backing fabric 11 x 9in (28 x 23cm)

❊ Cream sewing cotton

❊ 1yd (1m) pre-gathered cream lace, 2in (5cm) wide

❊ Polyester filling

❊ 18in (46cm) very narrow pink ribbon

❊ Use two strands of stranded cotton (floss) over two threads of linen throughout.

1 Follow steps 1 and 2 for the Wedding Ring Sampler (page 70) but omit the verse and work over two threads with two strands of cotton.

2 Cut the ribbon in half, thread through the fabric just underneath the embroidered bow as shown in the photograph (use a needle with a large eye to thread the ribbon through). Leave the ends trailing at this stage.

3 Trim the embroidered fabric to within 1½in (4cm) of the work and cut the backing fabric to the same size.

4 Machine or hand stitch the two short ends of the lace together and either oversew or zigzag to neaten. Pin and tack (baste) the gathered edge of the lace, with right sides facing, to the embroidered fabric.

5 Making sure that the frilled edge of the lace is pointing towards the centre of the work (you may like to tack (baste) this edge down so that it does not catch in the seam), place the backing fabric right side facing on top of the work, matching the edges together. Pin, tack (baste) and then machine stitch through all layers ½in (1.5cm) from the edge, leaving a 2in (5cm) opening for turning. Remove the tacking (basting) stitches. Turn through to the right side, and after filling close the opening with invisible stitches.

6 Add the wedding rings tied with a bow with the trailing ribbons – probably safer to do this at the last minute at the church!

ABCDEFGHIJ
KLM
NOP
QR
ST
UVWXYZ
ABCDEFGHIJK
LMNOPQRSTUV
WXYZ
ABCDEFGHIJKLMN
OPQRSTUVWXYZ
BK

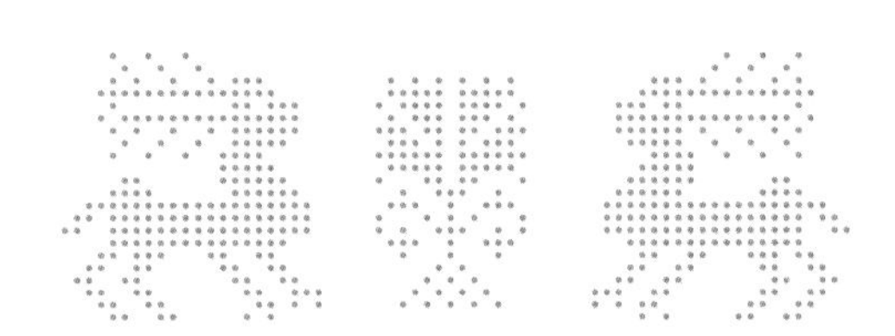

FLORA AND FAUNA SAMPLERS

Plants and animals, in all their wondrous variance, have contributed greatly to the embroiderers' palette of design possibilities for centuries past, offering those with the skill and imagination a cornucopia of ideas. Plants and animals, more than any other subject have been the favoured choice of sampler makers. Just as we do today, the early embroiderer would study books on horticulture as a source of inspiration. Borders in particular have benefited from the wealth of diversification the plant world has to offer.

The strawberry was a very popular choice, as was the acorn. Honeysuckle, roses and carnations were also firm favourites, but there surely cannot have been a tree, shrub or flower that has not appeared on a sampler in some guise or other. Oversized flowering shrubs in ornamental pots were a firm choice as the focus of many a sampler design, and appeared profusely on samplers across the ages – most with scant regard for scale. Trees, (especially the oak, much favoured in the restoration period, as Charles II was said to have hid in one in a bid to escape from the Puritan army in 1651), have appeared in all shapes and sizes; mainly symmetrical and in ordered rows, but some with a pretence of realism.

Weeping willows were often worked in satin stitch, and featured extensively on mourning samplers after the deaths of Princess Charlotte in 1817, and later Prince Albert in 1861. Animals – lions, stags, squirrels, rabbits – and almost every variety of bird known to man, have appeared on samplers, sometimes symbolically. Lions for example denoted strength; rabbits, gentleness; and squirrels, mischief. Facing birds often accompanied a plant in a pot, tree, or flowering shrub, and rows of birds were very common. The world of nature has, and always will be a constant source of fascination and inspiration to the embroiderer.

Left Four Flora and Fauna Miniatures, page 103.

The Becky Knole Sampler

The original Becky Knole sampler is very different to the one shown here. I bought it many years ago in a very sad and dusty condition simply because I liked some of the motifs it contained. I have kept and repeated some of them, changed the colour scheme, altered the border and the overall shape and now very little remains of Becky's original work, although I like to think the conversion may have pleased her. Parts of this sampler are worked in Marlitt thread which gives a lovely sheen, particularly in the sawtooth/satin stitch border.

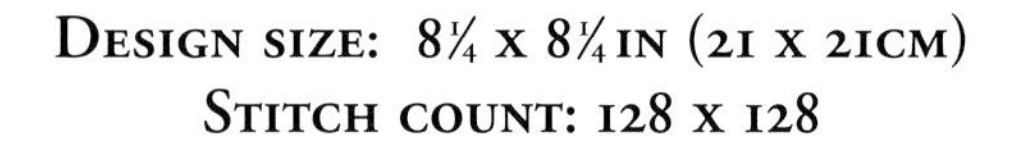

Design size: 8¼ x 8¼in (21 x 21cm)
Stitch count: 128 x 128

❋ 12 x 12in (30.5 x 30.5cm) cream Belfast linen, 32 threads per inch (2.5cm)

❋ Stranded cottons (floss) as shown in the key

❋ Marlitt viscose thread No. 1012

❋ Use two strands of stranded cotton (floss) and one strand of Marlitt thread over two threads of linen for the border, main alphabet, 'Anno Domini' and date. Work the remainder of the design with one strand of stranded cotton (floss) over one thread of linen. Use two strands of Marlitt for the sawtooth/satin stitch border.

1 It is usually suggested that you start work at the centre of the design but here it is more practical to complete all the work over two threads first as this will aid the correct placement of the inner motifs which are worked over just one thread. Measure 2¼in (6cm) down and 6in (15cm) in from the side of your fabric and begin working the top middle strawberry motif here in cross stitch.

2 The raised effect of the main alphabet, Anno Domini, and the date is achieved by working padded cross stitch – this is a simple cross stitch with another cross worked on top of it (see Stitch Library page 12). This will make the letters stand proud of the design, giving the appearance of tiny beads.

3 Stretch, mount and frame as required (see pages 137–139 for advice).

See how the lilies flourish
wite and faire,
See how the ravens fed from heaven are;
Never distrust thy God
for cloth and bread
While lilies flourish and the
raven's fed.

Becky

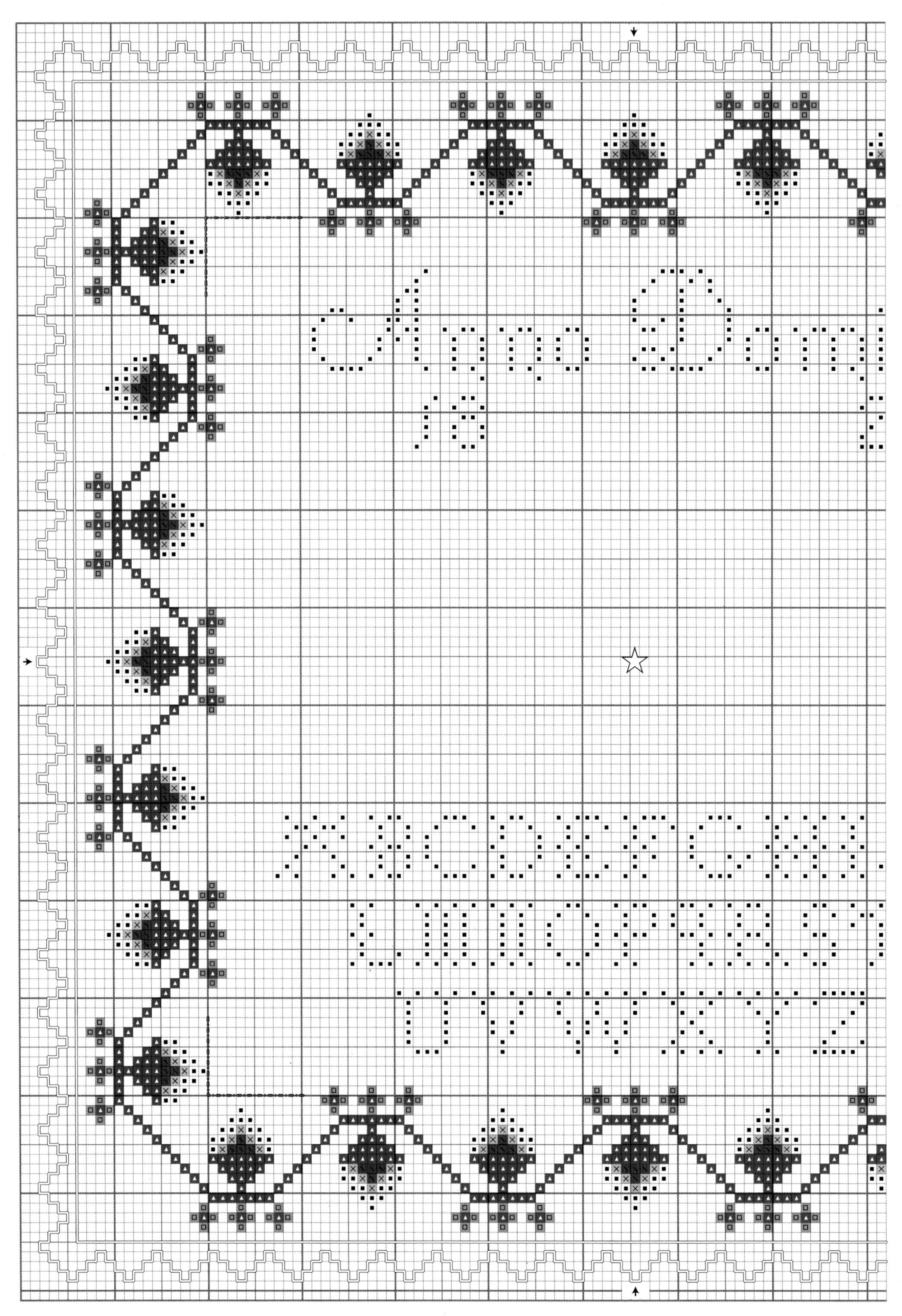

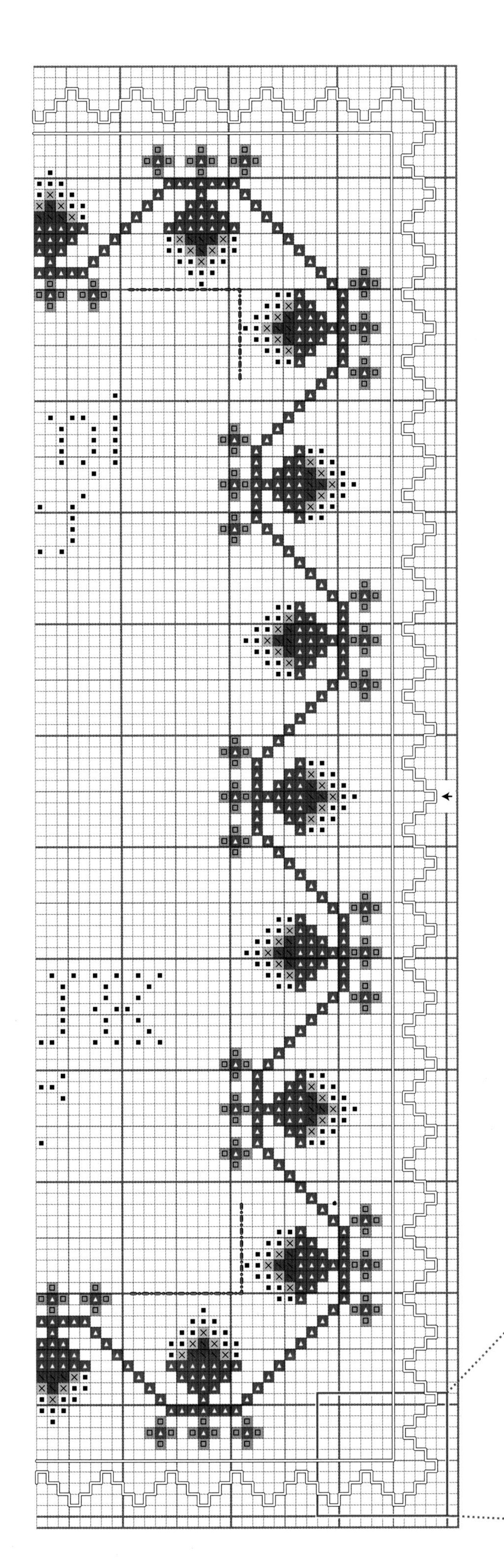

Becky Knole Sampler

DMC

- 500 very dark green
- 733 light sage
- 912 maroon
- 842 light beige
- 223 deep pink
- 407 pink beige

- Marlitt 1012 light cream

Motifs are worked over one thread.
Match centre 'star' and work
the floral basket here.
Position all other motifs as shown
on the additional chart

Detail of sawtooth border with mitred corner – satin stitch worked with 2 strands Marlitt 1012 light cream

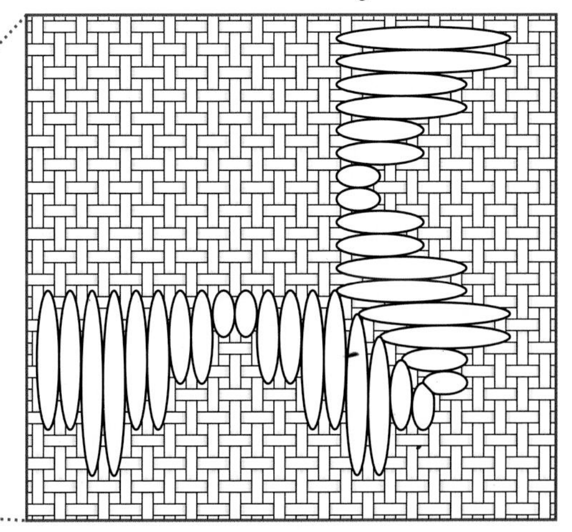

Becky

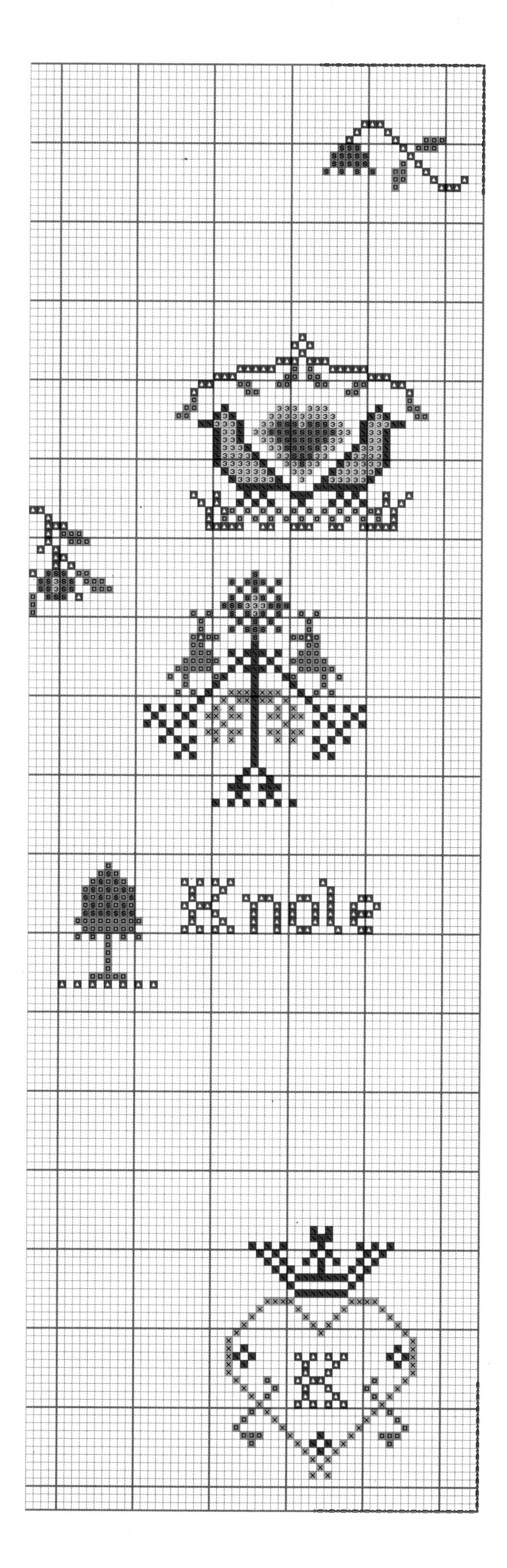

Becky Knole Sampler

DMC

- 500 very dark green
- 733 light sage
- 912 maroon
- 842 light beige
- 223 deep pink
- 407 pink beige

- Marlitt 1012 light cream

Motifs are worked over one thread.
Match centre 'star' and work
the floral basket here.
Position all other motifs as shown
on the additional chart

Carnations Sampler

The wonderfully rich colours of the carnations in the border of this design set the scene for the rest of the work. Carnations have been featured on samplers throughout the centuries. Symbolically, they are associated with maternal love and so are particularly appropriate for a home based sampler. Flower pots were commonly used on samplers of all types, with typical disregard for scale. The brightness of the colours would not have been unusual for samplers worked in the past. The soft, faded colours we now associate with traditional samplers are just that – soft and faded. The original shades would have been far more vivid.

DESIGN SIZE: 15½ x 12¼ IN (39 x 31CM)
STITCH COUNT: 205 x 155

❊ 20 x 17in (51 x 43cm) natural Dublin linen, 25 threads per inch (2.5cm)

❊ Stranded cottons (floss) as shown in the key

❊ Use two strands of stranded cotton (floss) over two threads of linen, except for the name which is worked with one strand over one thread.

1 Find the centre of the design and work outwards from this point in cross stitch following the chart.

2 If you wish to personalise the sampler, work out the name, date and so on, in pencil on graph paper (additional alphabets can be found on page 135), and then position as shown on the chart.

3 Stretch, mount and frame as required (see pages 137–139 for advice).

ABCDEFGHIJKLMN
OPQRSTUVWXYZ
Abigail Markham
18
21

Carnations Sampler

DMC

Symbol	DMC
▪▪	310 black
▮▮	347 red
× ×	3051 mid green
T T	890 dark green
▲▲	300 chocolate brown
S S	680 gold
= =	744 light yellow

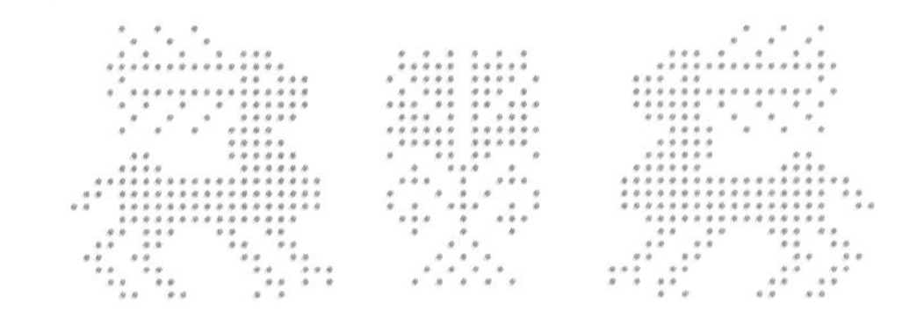

Birds Sampler

Birds have featured on samplers from the early seventeenth century, usually atop a bush, tree, or house; sometimes in rows, or as a single decorative motif. The border for this sampler is based on a Dutch design dated 1843. It is unusual for such big birds to play as large a part as this in a border design, but symmetrically placed they give a wonderful sense of balance to an already pretty border.

Design size: 10½ x 13½in (27 x 34cm)
Stitch count: 159 x 209

❊ 15 x 18in (38 x 46cm) cream Belfast linen, 32 threads per inch (2.5cm)

❊ Stranded cottons (floss) as shown in the key

❊ Use two strands of stranded cotton (floss) over two threads of linen, except for the verse and name which are both worked with one strand of 310 black over one thread of linen. For the verse and name, follow the charts on page 102. The first letter of each line of text is also charted on the main chart on page 100 to help you position the letters correctly.

1 Find the centre of the design and work in cross stitch from this point following the chart.

2 If you wish to substitute your own name, year and so on, work out your details in pencil on graph paper (using the alphabets and numerals from the additional alphabets on page 135), and position as shown on the chart.

3 Stretch, mount and frame as required (see pages 137–139 for advice).

'Missing' Letters

The letters I, J, M, U, V or W are sometimes missing on antique samplers especially early examples. There are a number of explanations for this occurrence. In the classical period, the Latin alphabet had only twenty-three letters, that is, the English alphabet without J, V and W. The letter V was the capital form of the letter u, but as u became more commonly employed as a consonant, it evolved into a distinct letter. The use of the letter J was not standard until the middle of the nineteenth century when Webster's dictionary was published. The J evolved from the letter I, which had been used only occasionally since the fourteenth century. Omission of certain letters saved labour for the stitcher. Marking samplers, which were worked as a visual example of letters to be copied onto household linen, and used as a working tool, often omitted letters which could be adapted from others – W from V; I from H; M from N.

The bird which soars on highest wing
Builds on the ground her lowly nest,
And she that doth most
sweetly sing
Sings in the shade when all things rest.
18
27
Lucy
Tyler

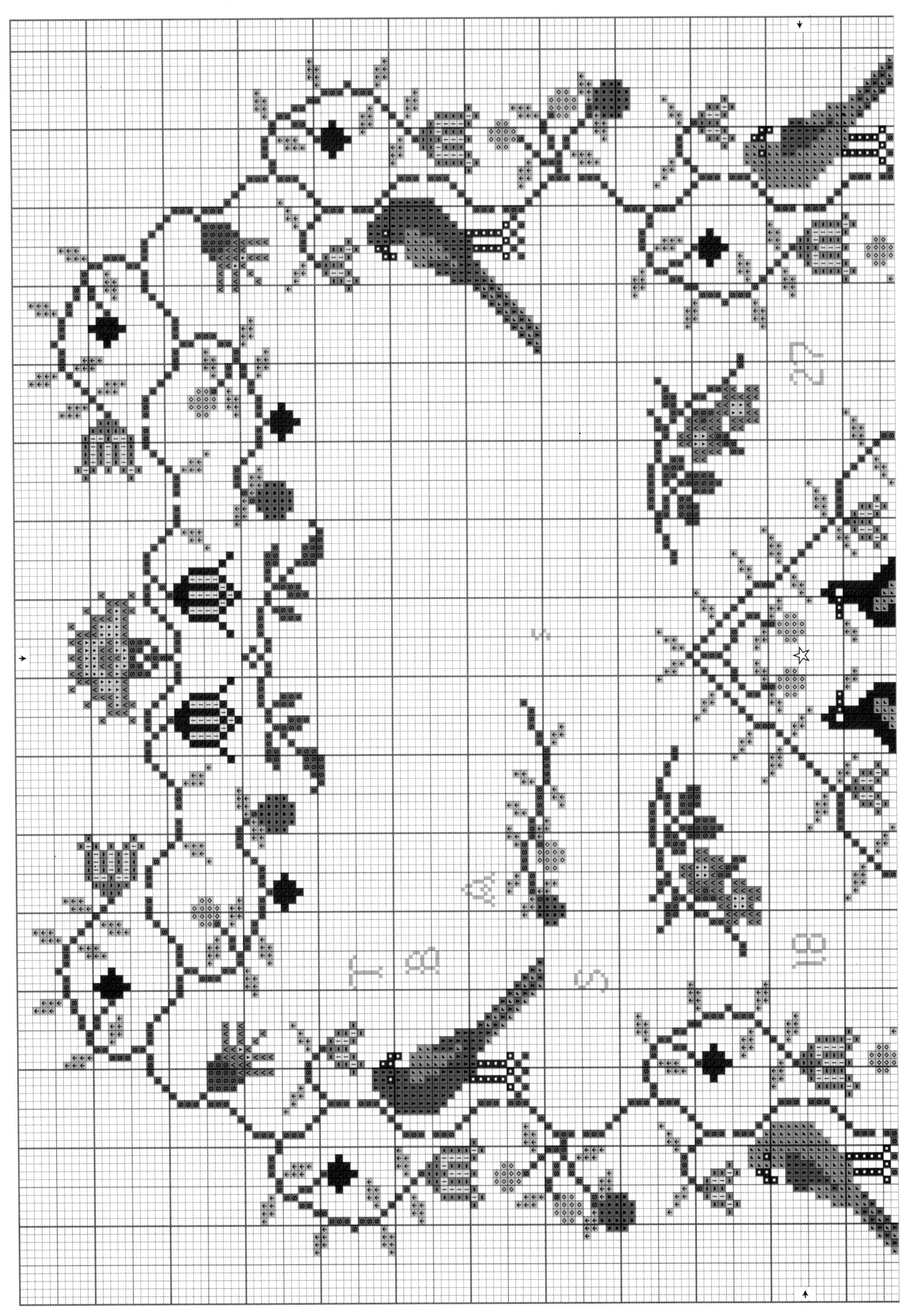

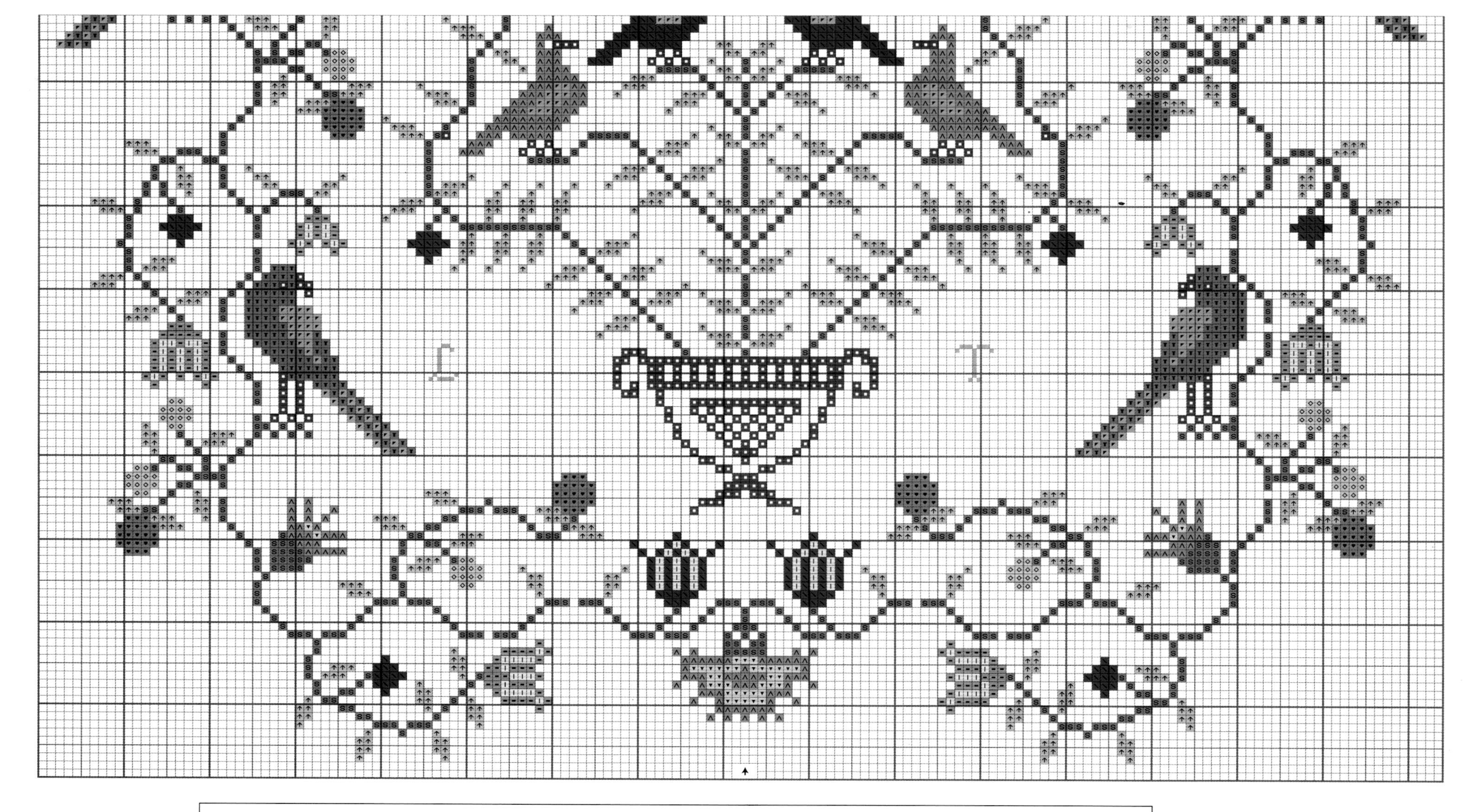

Birds Sampler

DMC

- 3371 very dark brown
- 924 antique blue
- 502 soft turquoise
- 355 rust
- 951 soft pink beige
- 730 dark sage green
- 733 light sage green
- 680 gold
- 738 light beige
- 3042 pale lilac
- 3041 dark lilac
- 356 apricot

Text
3371 very dark brown cross stitch over 1 thread with 1 strand

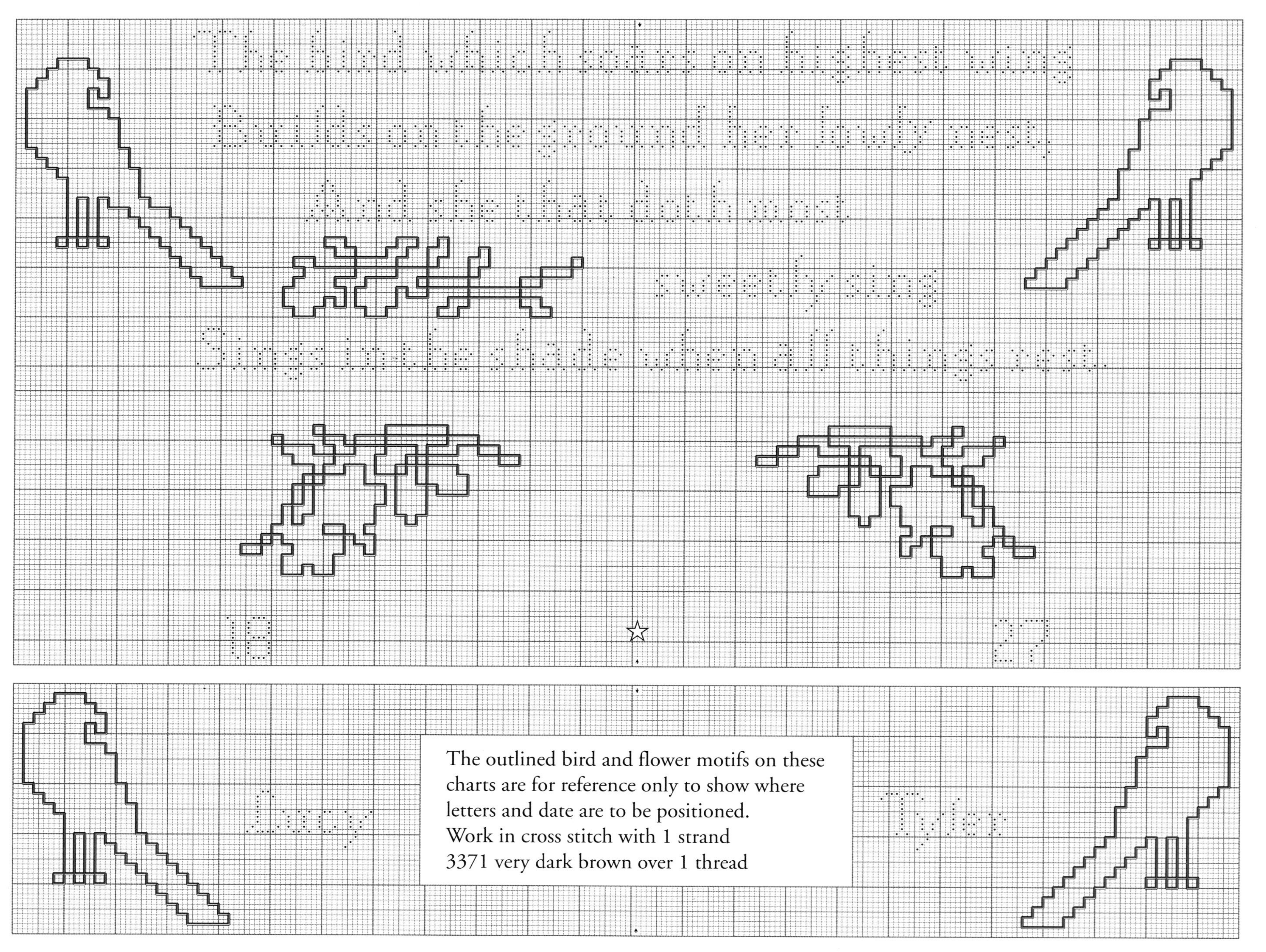
The bird which soars on highest wing
Builds on the ground her lowly nest,
And she that doth most
sweetly sing
Sings in the shade when all things rest.
18
27
Lucy
Tyler
The outlined bird and flower motifs on these charts are for reference only to show where letters and date are to be positioned.
Work in cross stitch with 1 strand
3371 very dark brown over 1 thread

Four Flora and Fauna Miniatures

This charming set of miniatures all share a common colour scheme, alphabet and border, and are positively awash with birds, animals, flowers and fruit. This set of designs (see photograph on page 86) clearly show how it is possible to decide on a theme, choose certain constants, and then develop it further by adding sympathetic elements to the design. It is an idea that I feel would work well with other themes – people or houses for example.

Squirrels Sampler
Design size: 5½ x 5½in (14 x 14cm)
Stitch count: 97 x 97

❋ 9 x 9in (23 x 23cm) 18 count Rustico fabric

❋ Stranded cotton (floss) as shown in the key

Lions Sampler
Design size: 3¾ x 6½in (9.5 x 16cm)
Stitch count: 66 x 114

❋ 7 x 10in (18 x 25.5cm) 18 count Rustico fabric

❋ Stranded cottons (floss) as shown in the key

Peacocks Sampler
Design size: 6½ x 3¾in (16.5 x 9.5cm)
Stitch count: 114 x 66

❋ 10 x 7in (25.5 x 18cm) 18 count Rustico fabric

❋ Stranded cottons (floss) as shown in the key

Stags Sampler
Design size: 4½ x 6¼in (11 x 16cm)
Stitch count: 78 x 108

❋ 8 x 10in (20 x 25.5cm) 18 count Rustico fabric

❋ Stranded cottons (floss) as shown in the key

For all 4 designs:
Use two strands of stranded cotton (floss) over one block of fabric.

1 Find the centre of the design and work outwards in cross stitch from this point following the chart.

2 If you wish to personalise any of the designs by substituting your own initials, use the alphabet given on the chart on page 104 and work out your details in pencil on graph paper and position as shown on the chart.

3 Stretch, mount and frame as required (see pages 137–139 for advice).

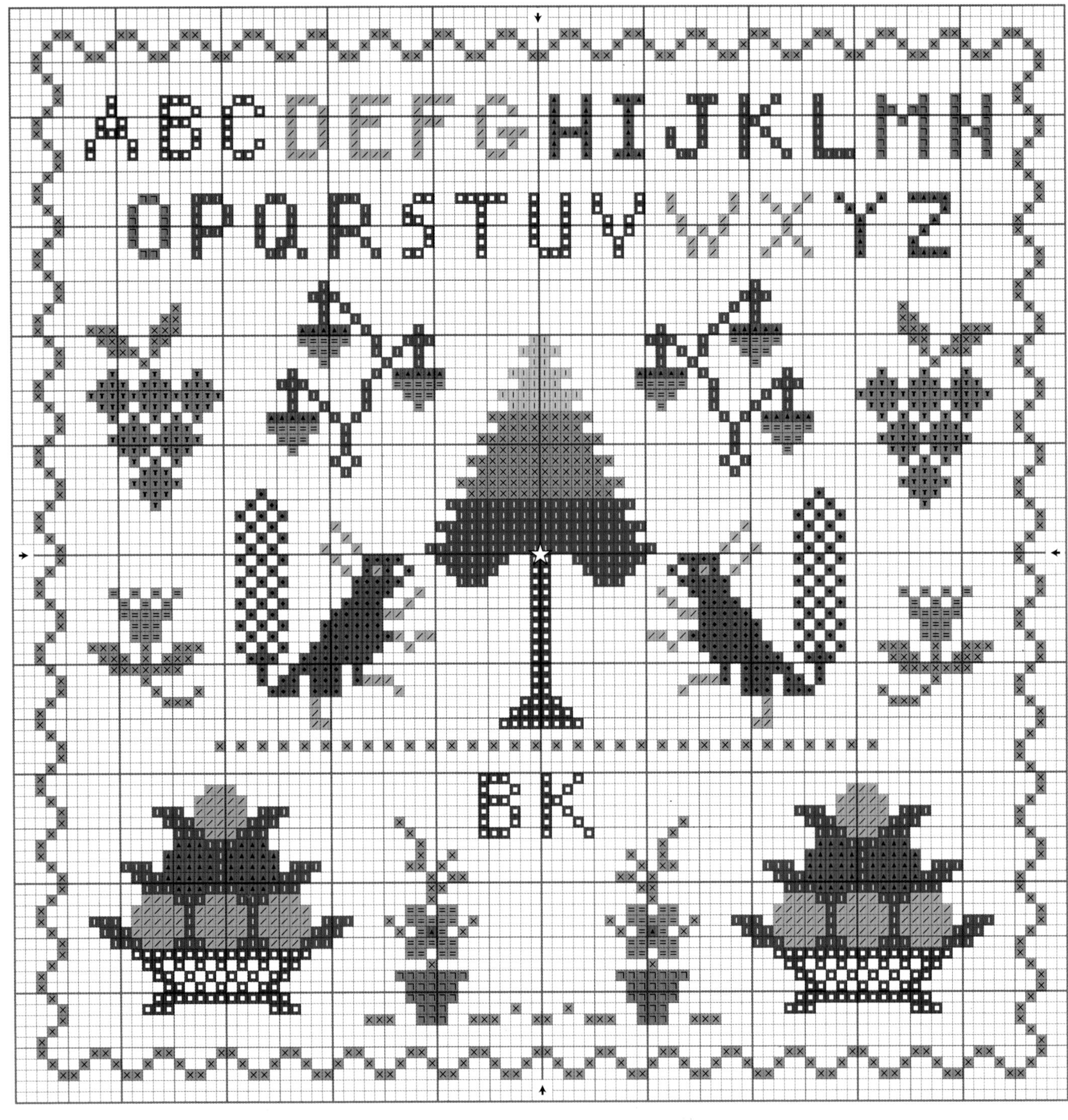

Squirrels *(above)* and Lions *(opposite)* Samplers

DMC

- 3371 very dark brown
- 434 warm brown
- 355 rust
- 356 apricot
- 730 dark sage green
- 890 dark green
- 680 gold
- 733 light sage green
- 3041 dark lilac
- 300 milk chocolate brown

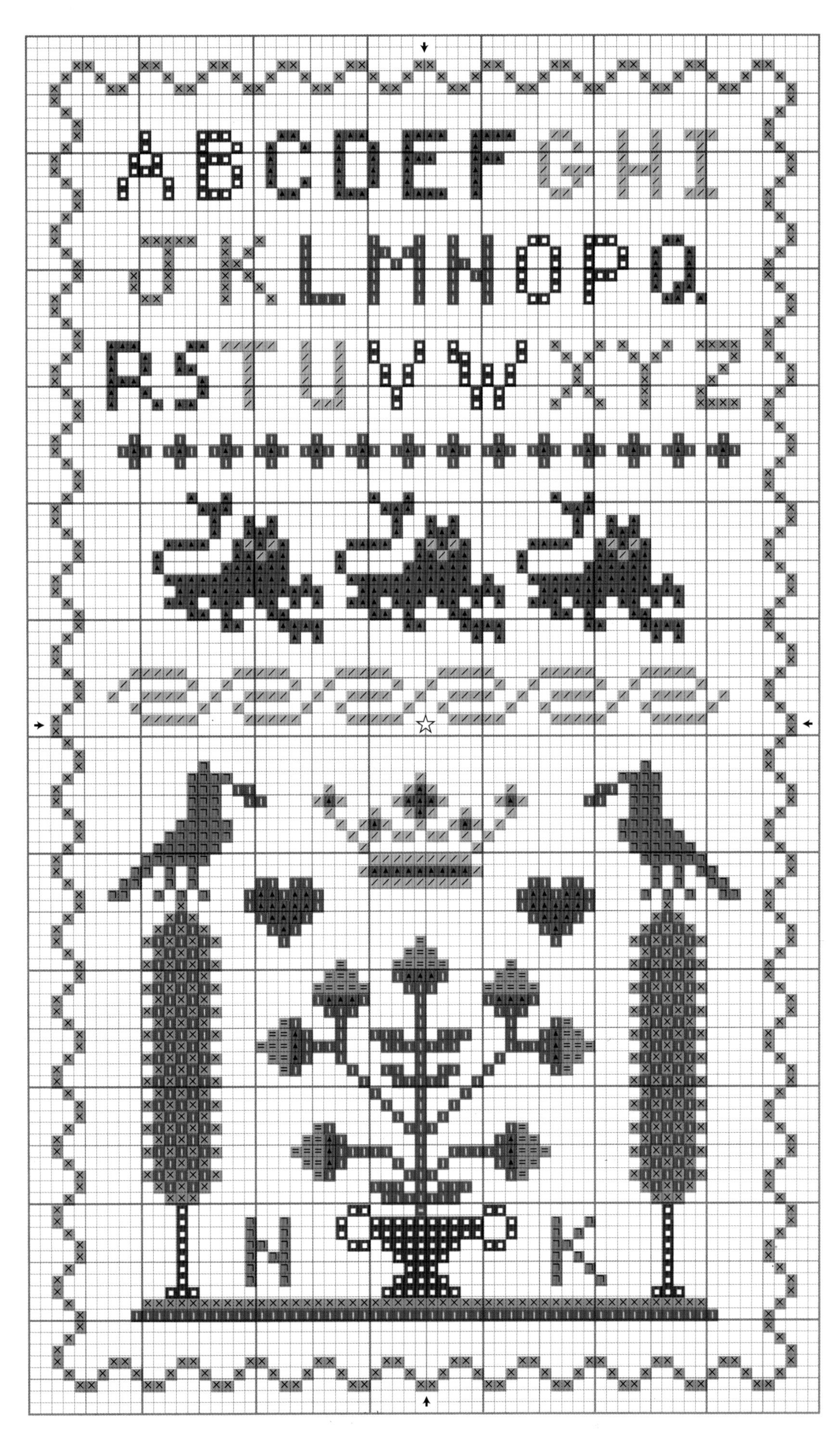

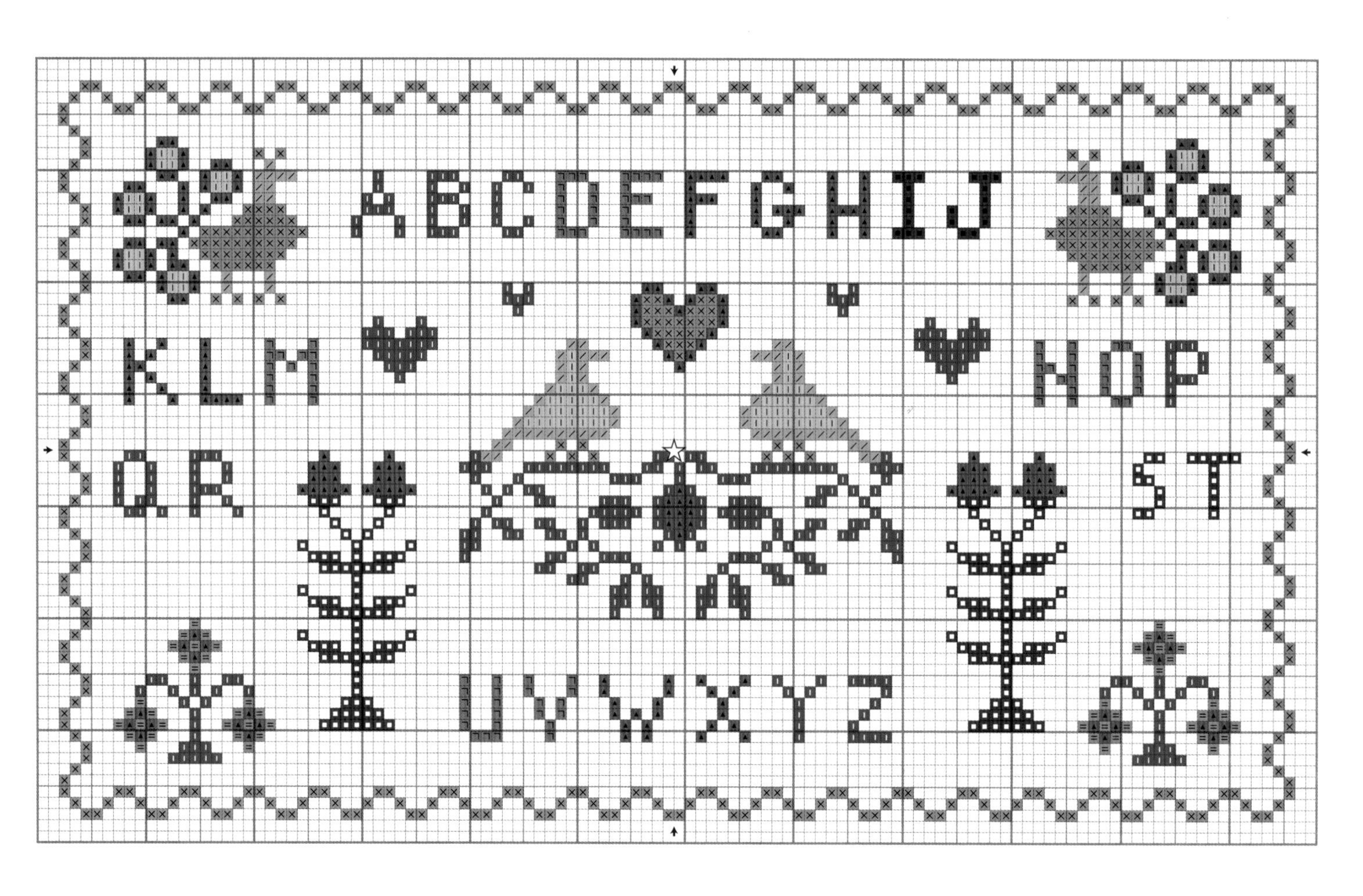

Peacocks *(above)*
and Stags *(opposite* **Samplers**

DMC

- 3371 very dark brown
- 434 warm brown
- 355 rust
- 356 apricot
- 730 dark sage green
- 890 dark green
- 680 gold
- 733 light sage green
- 3041 dark lilac
- 300 milk chocolate brown

Miniature Samplers

Genuine antique miniature samplers are a very rare find and much to be prized. Most can be categorised as 'marking samplers', featuring alphabets and numerals and worked in one colour. It is probable to assume that they were either a beginner's introduction to the art of sampler making, or more likely, a useful utilitarian working sampler to aid the marking of household linen – hence 'marking sampler'. Some of the more elaborate examples were obviously destined as gifts for special friends or relatives, and often included a short verse and the name of either the maker, recipient, or both.

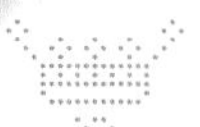

ABCDEFGHIJK
LMNOPQRSTUV
WXYZ
C
K

Abigail Markham
1821
A M
18 21
B K
B K

ADDITIONAL PROJECTS

** The distinctive Abigail Markham Silhouette features the shrub in a pot from the Carnations Sampler (chart, page 96). It is worked with a variety of stitches and shows the versatility of a decorative motif – a technique that could be applied to many of the designs in this book. The silhouette is worked on cream 28 count evenweave linen, using two strands of 310 black stranded cotton (floss). Work the leaves in tent stitch over one thread of fabric (ie, a block of four stitches to every symbol). The remainder of the design is worked over two threads of fabric. Work the flowers in four-sided stitch, the flower pot in padded cross stitch, (see Becky Knole sampler, page 88) and the stalk, stem, initials and date in cross stitch (see Stitch Library page 12).*

** The Small Abigail Markham Sampler is also taken from the Carnations Sampler (chart, page 96) and uses the smaller border as a surround. Most of the larger samplers could be successfully reduced in size in this way. The small sampler (see chart page 111) is worked in cross stitch on beige 28 count Quaker cloth, using two strands of stranded cotton (floss) over two threads of linen.*

** The Bird Picture housed in the gold frame and the red Birds Silhouette, are both taken from the larger Birds Sampler (chart, page 100). Both designs would make wonderful cards. The Bird Picture is worked in cross stitch on cream 28 count evenweave, using two strands of stranded cotton (floss) over two threads of linen. The Birds Silhouette is worked in tent stitch on cream 32 count Belfast linen, using two strands of 347 dull red stranded cotton (floss) over one thread of linen.*

** The Pincushion design is taken from the Becky Knole Sampler (chart, page 90–93) and is housed in a round wooden pincushion base. It is worked in cross stitch on beige 28 count Quaker cloth, using two strands of stranded cotton (floss) over two threads of linen. This design would also be ideal as a card.*

** The Floral Pot Picture, also from the Becky Knole Sampler (chart, page 90–93), makes a wonderful framed picture, or you could try working the design in wool on a larger mesh canvas for a cushion. It is worked in cross stitch on cream 28 count Quaker cloth, using two strands of stranded cotton (floss) over two fabric threads.*

Above The Lion Box Lid and Golden Lions Picture

* *The Facing Birds Pot Lid uses elements from the peacocks sampler in the Four Flora and Fauna Miniatures project (chart, page 106) as a design for a wooden trinket pot lid. It is worked in tent stitch on cream 32 count Belfast linen, using two strands of stranded cotton (floss) over one thread of linen.*

* *The single lion from the lions sampler in the Four Flora and Fauna Miniatures has also inspired this simple but elegant Lion Box Lid (above). The design, worked in cross stitch on 14 count gold-coloured stitching paper, uses two strands of 939 navy stranded cotton (floss) over one block of paper. Follow the Golden Lions chart on page 111, working only one lion centrally.*

* *Four lions, worked in cross stitch in gold thread on navy 14 count Aida, have been framed to form this Golden Lions Picture (above), but would also make a wonderful decoration for a square box lid.*

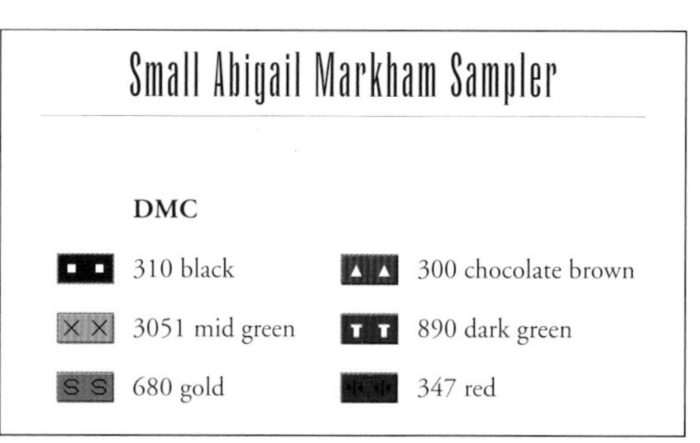

Small Abigail Markham Sampler

DMC

310 black	300 chocolate brown
3051 mid green	890 dark green
680 gold	347 red

Golden Lions Picture

DMC 282 gold thread

BETHANY
25 Aug 1998
ABCDEFGHIKL
MNOPQRSTUV
WXYZ
Emma & Christopher Marsh
Born 14th April 1998
ABCDEFGHIJKLMNOP
PATRICK
18·5·1998

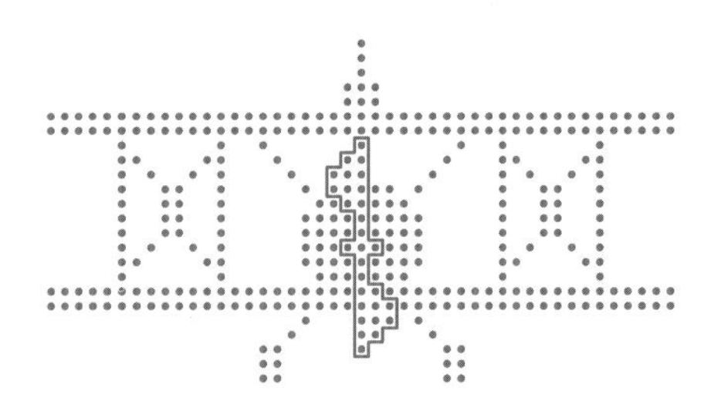

A CELEBRATION OF CHILDHOOD

The only dated sampler known to have survived from the sixteenth century records the birth of a child. The inscription on the sampler reads as follows:

ALICE : LEE : WAS : BORNE : THE : 23: OF : NOVEMBER : BE ING : TWESDAY: IN : THE : AFTER : NOONE : 1596

The Jane Bostocke sampler of 1598 is therefore, the first surviving sampler to celebrate the birth of a child.
Samplers recording the births and deaths of whole families were far more common during the last five centuries than ones which recorded a single birth. It is a sad testament of the times that many families lost loved ones at an early age, and were understandably keen to preserve their memory in a loving and lasting memorial.
The present generation of stitchers are, happily, able to devote their time and creative energies to stitching works of embroidery which celebrate life's joyous occasions. The birth of a child in particular, seems to engender in us all the need to give a meaningful gift. Christening or birth samplers are the perfect choice, as they are sure to be treasured for the life time of the recipient. More than likely they will then be passed down as treasured heirlooms. Samplers stitched with love and affection as a birth or christening gift, are therefore very prized indeed, and worth every minute of the time and skill dedicated to them.

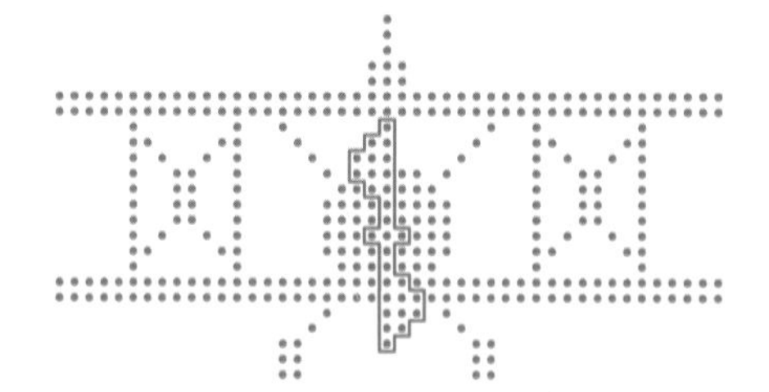

Whitework Christening Sampler

What more appropriate gift could a loving godparent (or indeed anyone) give than this exquisite whitework christening sampler showing not only love but commitment and continuity. This sampler, worked with many stitches including satin stitch, Algerian eye, cross stitch, backstitch and four-sided stitch, is sure to be treasured. A variety of white and cream threads create differing textures within the design, and the use of silver thread in the border adds a touch of luxury.

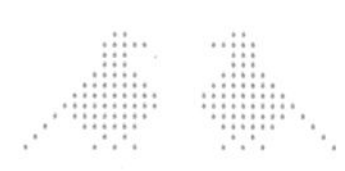

Design size: 7 x 9¼in (18 x 23cm)
Stitch count: 128 x 170

- 11 x 14in (28 x 36cm) cream Dublin linen, 25 threads per inch (2.5cm)
- Stranded cotton (floss) as shown in the key
- Marlitt threads as shown in the key
- Flower threads as shown in the key
- Perlé cotton No. 5 as shown in the key
- DMC D281 silver thread
- The main chart (page 116) has numbered rows 1 to 7 which refer to specific stitches. To work these, follow the instructions with the detailed stitch figures on page 117, referring also to the Stitch Library on page 12.

To stitch the commemorative lettering (no. 7), follow the chart and the key on page 117. The first letter of each row is charted on the main chart to help you position the words correctly.

1 Find the centre of the design and work outwards from this point following the chart.

2 To personalise the sampler, work out names, dates and so on using the alphabet and numerals from the additional alphabets on page 135. Work out your details in pencil on graph paper and position as shown on the chart.

3 Stretch, mount and frame as required (see pages 137–139 for advice).

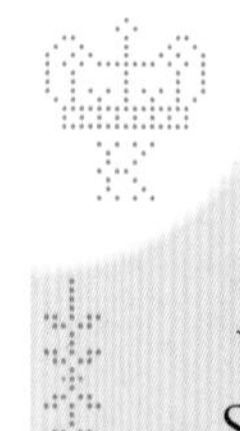

How happy is the lovely child
Of manners gentle, temper mild
Who learns each useful pretty art
Sure pleasure to her friends impart
Tis thus my parents sweeten toil
And my reward is in your smile.

To celebrate the
Christening of

1
2
3
4
5
6
7
Work letters in cross stitch with 1 strand
DMC Flower thread 2745 pale cream over 1 thread

Eyelet in DMC silver thread –
1 strand over 4 threads,
4-sided stitch in DMC
Perlé cotton No. 5 ecru –
1 strand over 4 threads

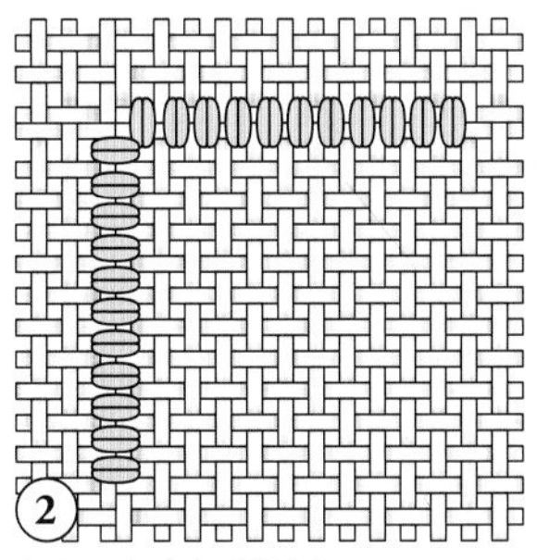

Satin stitch in DMC ecru –
2 threads pulled tight

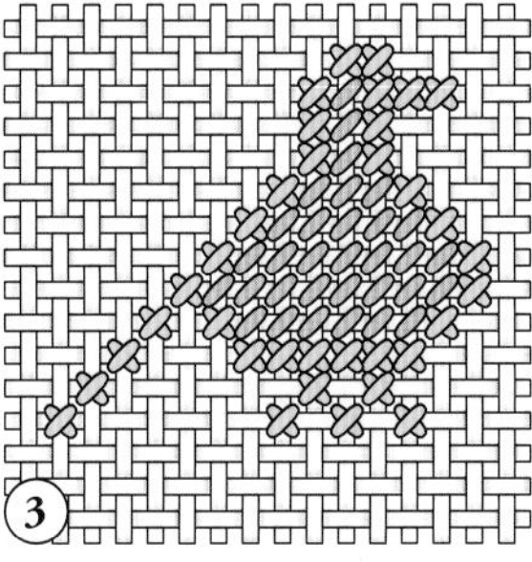

Cross stitch in DMC
Flower thread 2745 –
1 strand over 1 thread,
Tent stitch in Anchor Marlitt 1012 –
1 strand over 1 thread

Eyelet in DMC blanc – 1 strand over 4 threads,
Anchor Marlitt 1012 – 1 strand over 2 threads

Satin stitch in Anchor Marlitt 1012 – 1 strand,
Tent stitch in Anchor Marlitt 800 – 2 strands over 1 thread,
Tent stitch in DMC blanc – 2 strands over 1 thread,
Cross stitch in DMC ecru – 1 strand over 1 thread

DMC Flower thread blanc – 2 strands over 4 threads

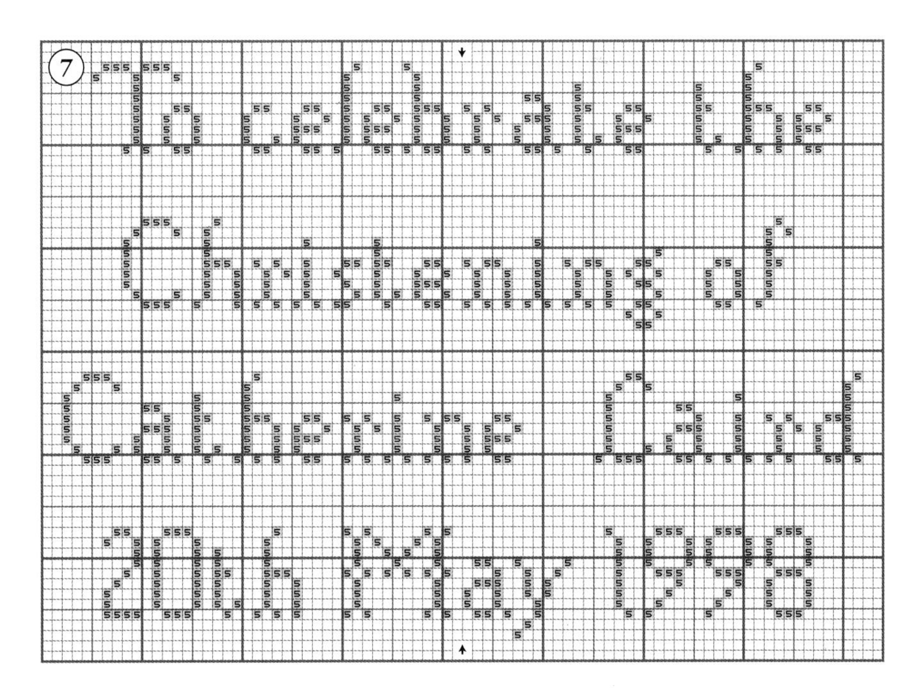

Whitework Christening Sampler

DMC

- ⊠ ⊠ DMC stranded cotton (floss) ecru
- 3 3 DMC stranded cotton (floss) blanc
- 5 5 DMC Flower thread 2745 pale cream
- – – DMC Flower thread blanc
- ◸ ◸ DMC silver thread D281
- Perle cotton No. 5 ecru
- ■ ■ Marlitt 800 white
- Marlitt 1012 cream

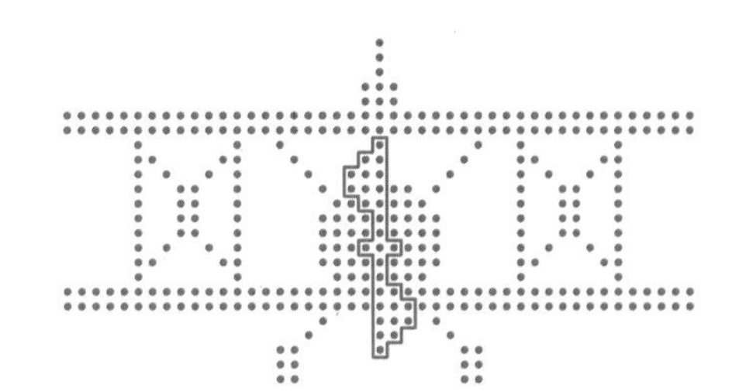

Edwardian-Style Birth Sampler

Bold in style with its imposing alphabet border and featuring many of the toys beloved in Edwardian times – tin soldiers, wooden biplane, kite, sailing ship – this colourful and unique sampler would make a welcome addition to the nursery. With the advent of the Edwardian era, 1901–1910, sampler making (with the exception of plain sewing samplers which were still made in schools up until the 1930s), had all but died out. This sampler therefore, is not meant to depict an 'Edwardian sampler' – in this format they simply did not exist. It is instead, a reflection of images from the period which convey the style of the times.

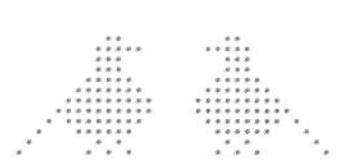

Design size: 12 x 9½in (30.5 x 24cm)
Stitch count: 163 x 129

- 16 x 14in (41 x 36cm) 14 count Rustico fabric
- Stranded cottons (floss) as shown in the key
- Use two strands of stranded cotton (floss) over one block of fabric throughout.

ABCDEFGHIJKLMNOP
PATRICK
18·5·1998
P
P
KLMNOPQRSTUVWXYZ
BRIGHTON

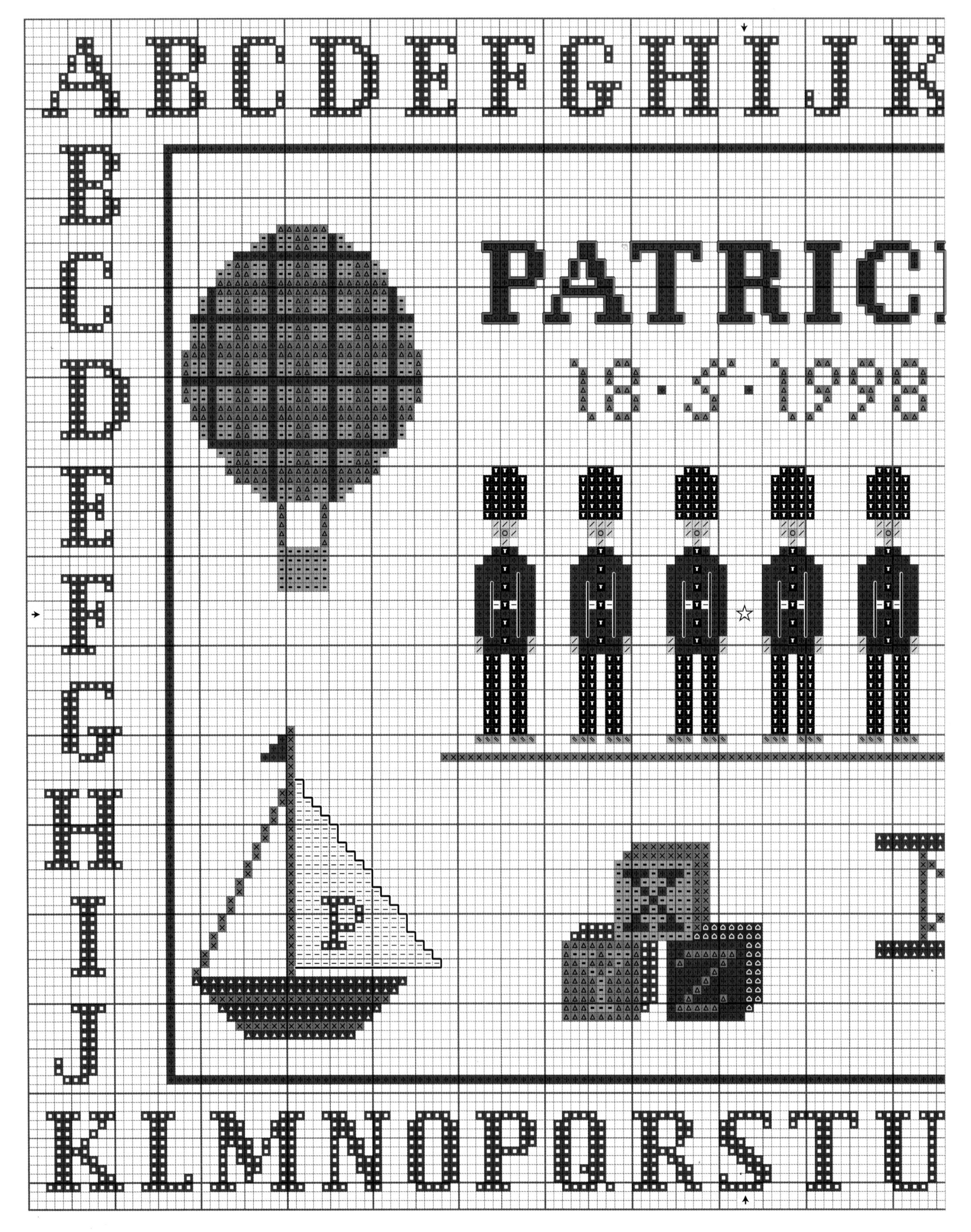

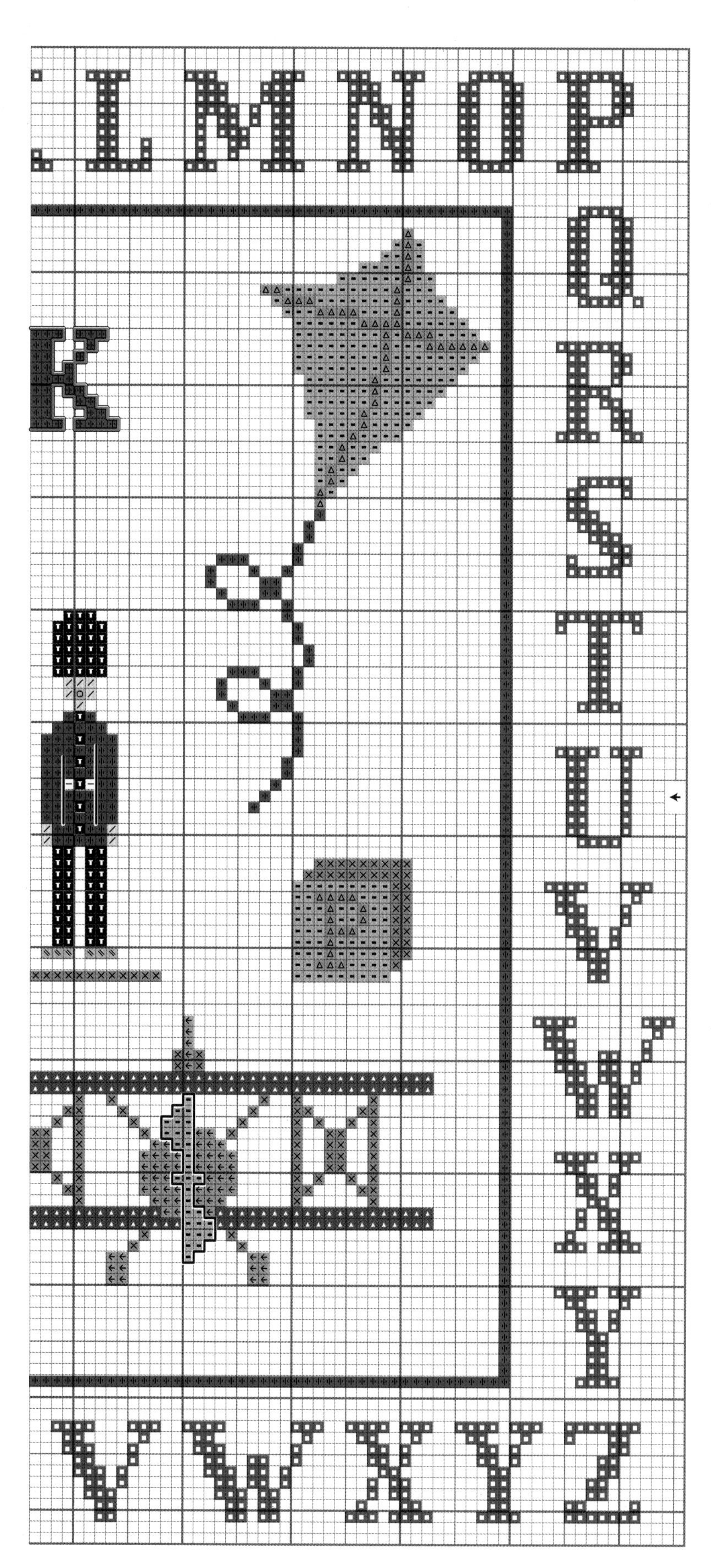

Edwardian-style Birth Sampler

DMC

- 310 black
- 317 dark grey
- ecru
- 3371 dark brown
- 434 warm brown
- 680 gold
- 823 navy
- 902 maroon
- 347 red
- 407 pink beige
- 400 rust
- 501 green blue
- 842 flesh

Backstitch

- 310 black use 1 strand to outline sail, propellor and add a backstitch line to soldiers arms (optional)
- 823 navy use 2 strands to outline name

1 Find the centre of the design and work outwards in cross stitch from this point following the chart.

2 To personalise the sampler, work out your name, date and so on using the alphabet from this chart or the additional alphabets and numerals on page 135. Work out your details in pencil on graph paper and position as shown on the chart.

3 Stretch, mount and frame as required (see pages 137–139 for advice).

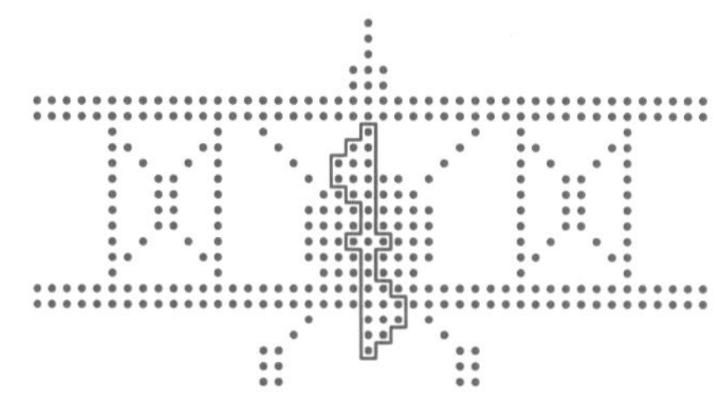

Twins Birth Sampler

The use of Watercolours thread by Caron gives an unusual slant to this traditional birth sampler. The children's initials contained in the interlocking hearts are left unworked, and the surrounding background filled with cross stitch worked in flower thread. The resulting flat, matt finish is a very effective contrast to the raised outline of the hearts which is worked in the thicker Watercolours thread. Approximately one in every eighty pregnancies results in twins, so what better way to record such a rare joyous event for posterity?

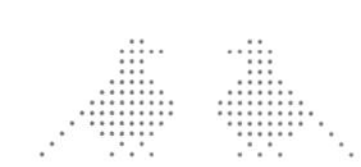

DESIGN SIZE: 14 x 14IN (36 x 36CM)
STITCH COUNT: 177 x 177

✻ 18 x 18in (46 x 46cm) cream Dublin linen, 25 threads per inch (2.5cm)

✻ Stranded cottons (floss) as shown in the key

✻ Caron Watercolours thread Confetti LC0281028

✻ DMC Flower thread 2396 lilac

✻ Use two strands of stranded cotton (floss), one strand of Watercolours and flower thread as it comes, over two threads of linen throughout.

1 Find the centre of the design and work outwards in cross stitch following the chart.

2 To personalise the sampler: if the twins are both girls, substitute the boy figure for another girl and vice versa for two boys swapping 'arms' in both cases to hold the ribbons. If the hair colour of the twins is dark, you could substitute brown or black thread in place of gold. Work out the names and date of birth in pencil on graph paper and then position as shown on the main chart. Use the large alphabet contained in the sampler for the capital letters (without the additional shading on the lettering) and the additional alphabet and numerals given on page 135 for the rest of the text.

3 Stretch, mount and frame as required (see pages 137–139 for advice).

Two sweet children, girl and boy
Shared each other's tears and joy,
They were ever side by side,
Like the Graces beautified.
Form without and thought within
Linked them by the name of twin
For the lips which smiled and burned
With the children's kiss returned.

Mary Diggle Aged 11 years 1852

ABCDEFGHIJKL
MNOPQRSTUV
WXYZ
Emma & Christopher Marsh
Born 14th April 1998

Emma & Christopher
Born 14th April

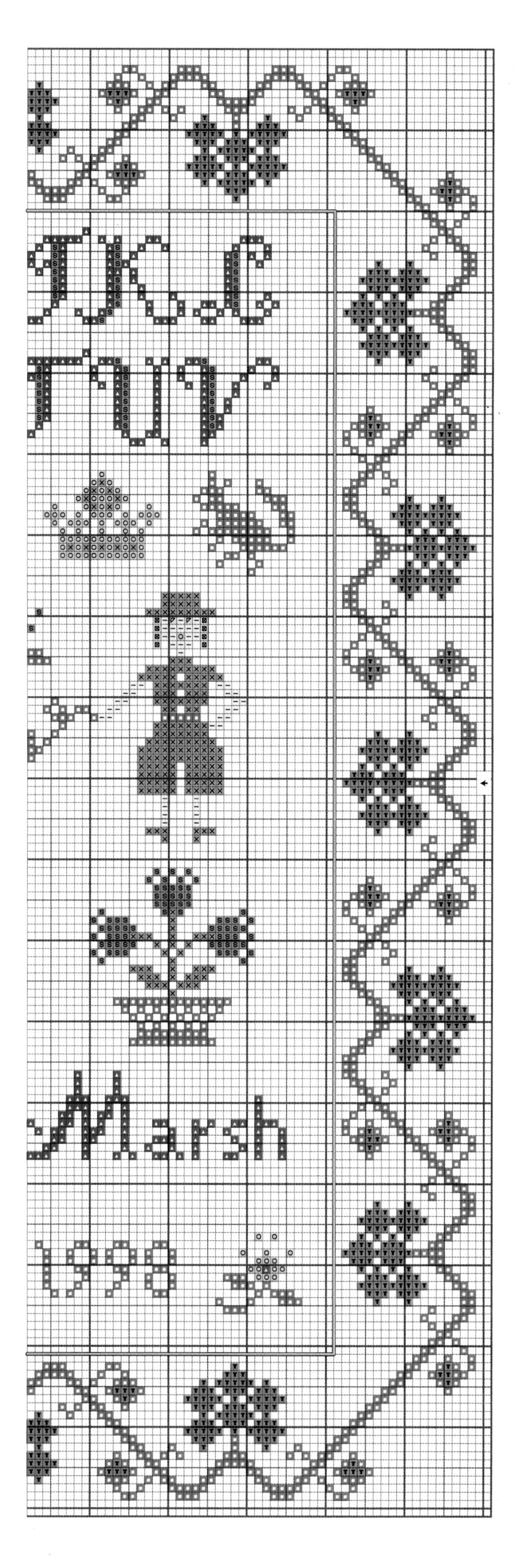

Twins Birth Sampler

DMC

- 842 flesh
- 761 light pink
- 927 light slate blue
- 502 blue green
- 223 strawberry pink
- 407 pink beige
- 501 dark blue green
- 745 yellow
- 315 plum

- Flower thread 2396 lilac

- Caron Watercolours Confetti LCO 281028

- Flower thread 2396 lilac

Little Girls Birth Sampler

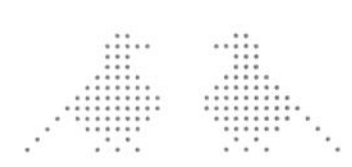

This sampler has a slightly more modern feel, although in the main, traditional motifs have been used. The mood I tried to create is light and pretty, even though the linen is a darker cream than the one I normally use. The effect of pale, subtle shades on the darker linen gives a lovely soft antique look to the design. The central theme is three little girls in a light-hearted game of skipping (although I am sure most mothers would throw up their hands in horror if their daughters attempted the same exercise in similar shoes!). An unusual alphabet with each individual letter tied up with a pretty bow is charted in full.

DESIGN SIZE: 10¾ x 10¾in (27 x 27cm)
STITCH COUNT: 153 x 153

❊ 15 x 15in (38 x 38cm) cream evenweave linen (Zweigart No. 233), 28 threads per inch (2.5cm)

❊ Stranded cottons (floss) as shown in the key

❊ Use two strands of stranded cotton (floss) over two threads of linen, except where indicated in the key.

1 Find the centre of the design and work outwards in cross stitch following the chart.

2 Work out your chosen name from the alphabet chart provided on page 129 in pencil on graph paper and then position on the main chart using the lines for guidance. Additional alphabets and numerals can be found on page 135. For accuracy I would recommend making a photocopy of the main chart and copying your design details onto this.

3 Stretch, mount and frame as required (see pages 137–139 for advice).

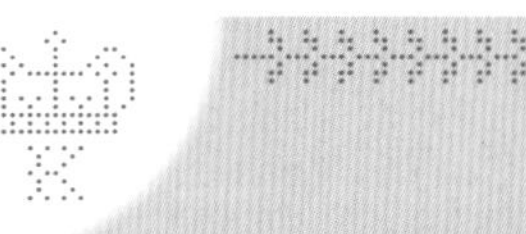

An inscription from a sampler dated 1797 reads:

'In reading this if any fault you see
Mend first your own and then find
fault in me.'

A defensive young soul clearly not enamoured with the subject!

ABCDEFGHIJK
LMNOPQRST
UVWXYZ
BETHANY
25 Aug 1998

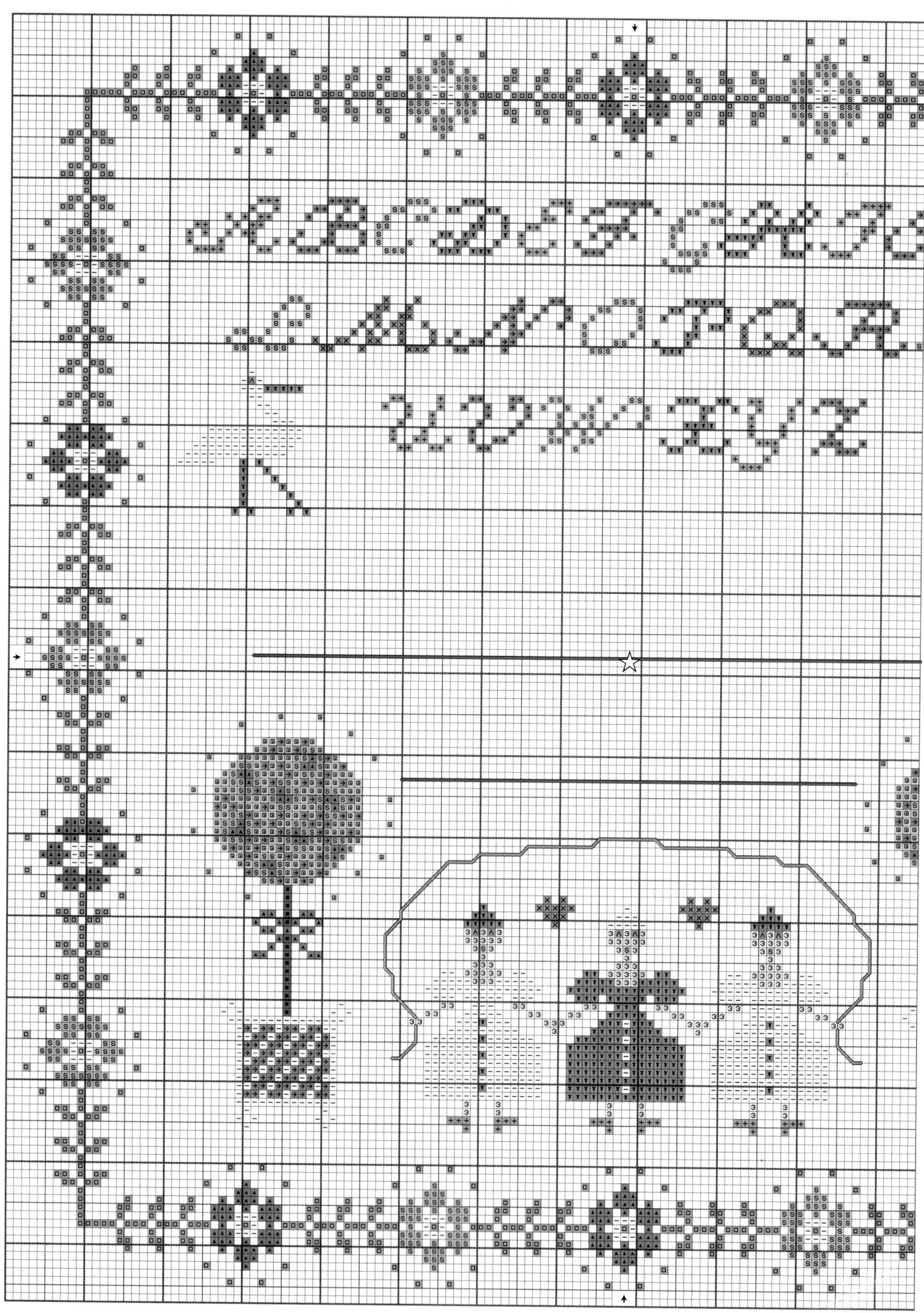

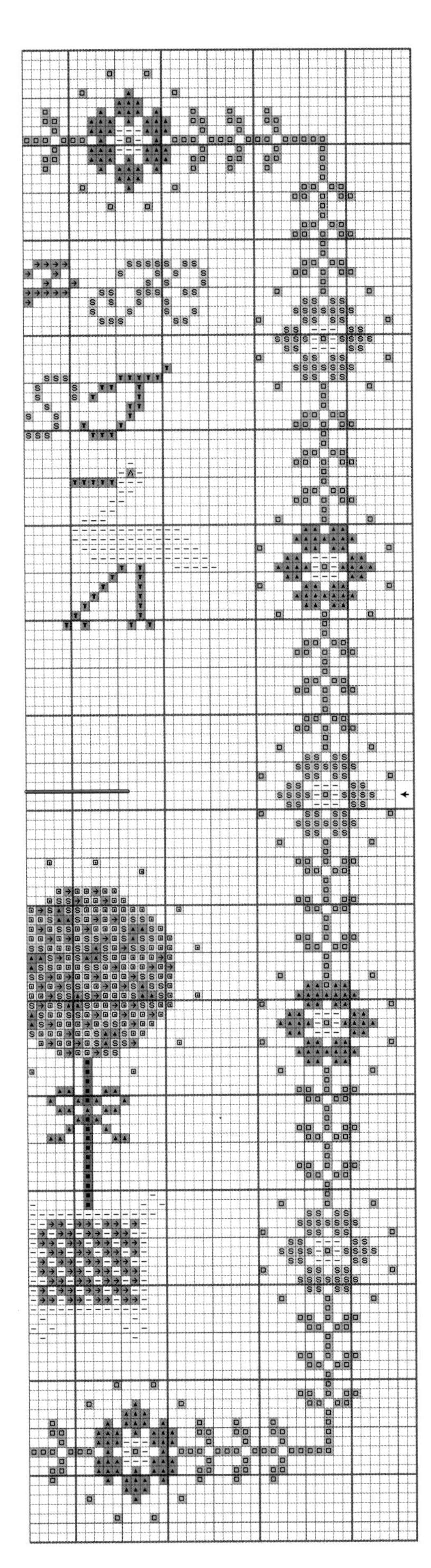

Little Girls Birth Sampler

DMC

- 3823 light cream
- 951 very pale pink
- 927 light slate blue
- 223 strawberry pink
- 760 deep pink
- 224 light pink
- 351 apricot pink
- 937 sage green
- 3052 mid green grey
- 3348 light grass green
- 3012 sage green
- 407 pink beige
- Skipping rope – work in backstitch with 2 strands 3012 sage green

Alphabet

- 3052 mid green grey
- 937 sage green
- 224 light pink
- 760 deep pink
- Outline bows on letters in backstitch with 1 strand 760 deep pink

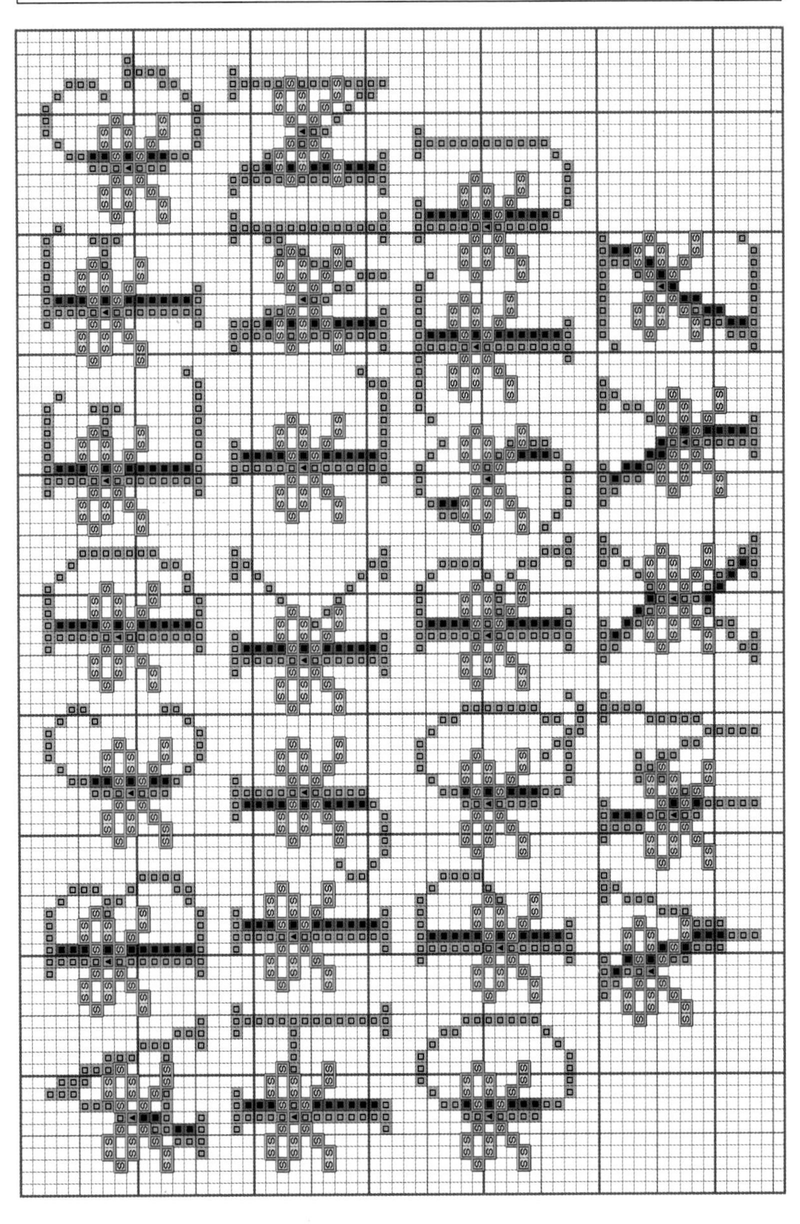

BETHANY
To celebrate the
Christening of
Catherine Caird
20th May 1998
ABCDEFG
P
P
Patrick
GFEDCBA

ADDITIONAL PROJECTS

Birth samplers probably more than any other type suggest possibilities for further projects. Shown here are just a few of the extra projects adapted from the larger designs. Alternative alphabets can be found on page 135.

✻ *The Little Girls Skipping picture (chart overleaf) is taken from the Little Girls Birth Sampler (page 126) and is worked in cross stitch in a single shade, ecru, on a rich plum background of 28 count Cashel linen (No. 483). Use two strands over two threads for the main part of the design and one strand over one thread for the name of your choice using the alphabet on page 128. The line on the chart is for guidance when placing the name of your choice. This design is very adaptable – why not try working it in space-dyed thread for example, and instead of a picture, make up the design as a small cushion to hang on a child's bedroom door.*

✻ *The Oval Birth Sampler though derived from the Twins Birth Sampler (page 122) is in complete contrast, using many differing shades of white and cream cross stitch on cream 28 count Dublin linen to add interest and texture. The heart motif surrounding the name could be used on its own as a design for a card. Narrow lace around the aperture of the card would add a special touch. The three lines within the heart motif are for guidance when placing the name of your choice (see alphabets on pages 135–136). Use two strands over two threads referring to the chart and key overleaf for specific instructions on thread use.*

✻ *The Boy's Name Picture is a smaller version of the Edwardian-Style Birth Sampler (page 118). 'Patrick' (chart page 133) is a bold and brightly coloured example of just how successfully a larger design can be reduced in size. It is worked in cross stitch on 18 count Rustico fabric, using two strands of stranded cotton (floss) over one block of fabric.*

✻ *The Small Christening Sampler, a smaller version of the Whitework Christening Sampler (page 114), is worked in tent stitch using three pastel shades on cream 32 count Belfast linen, with two strands of stranded cotton (floss) over one thread of fabric. This design is relatively quick to work and therefore perfect for a last minute gift. A trick I have used before is to buy a pretty and unusual frame (and/or mount) and then design the project to fit, as in this case.*

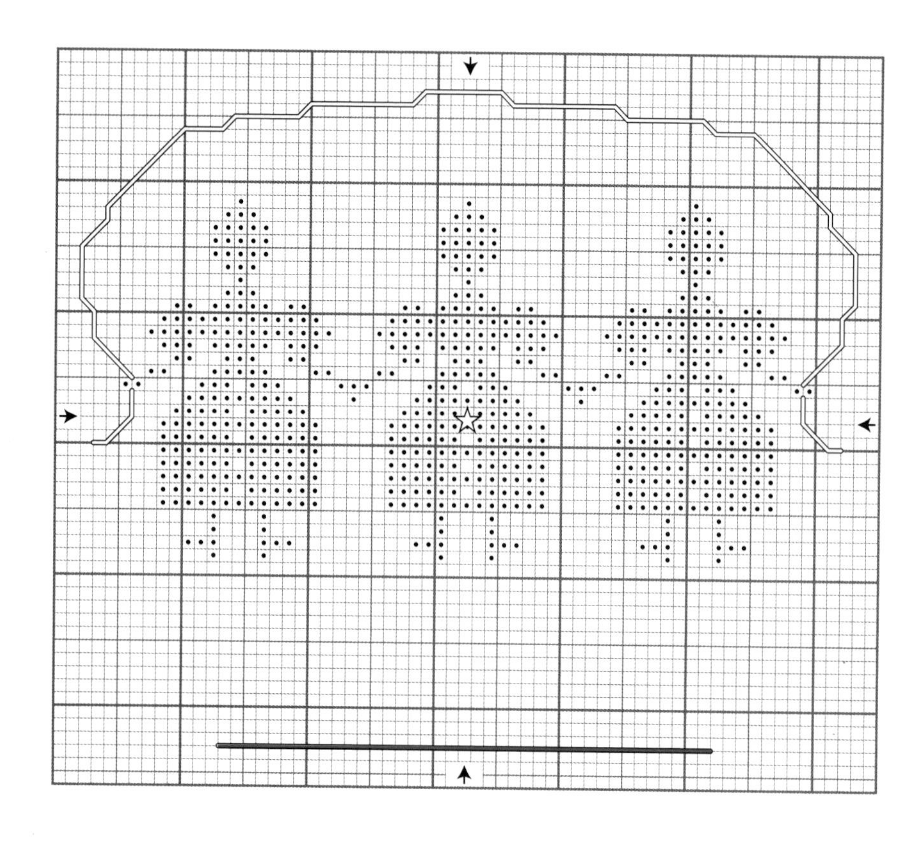

Little Girls Skipping

DMC

• • ecru

Backstitch skipping rope, ecru

Position name on ▬▬ line

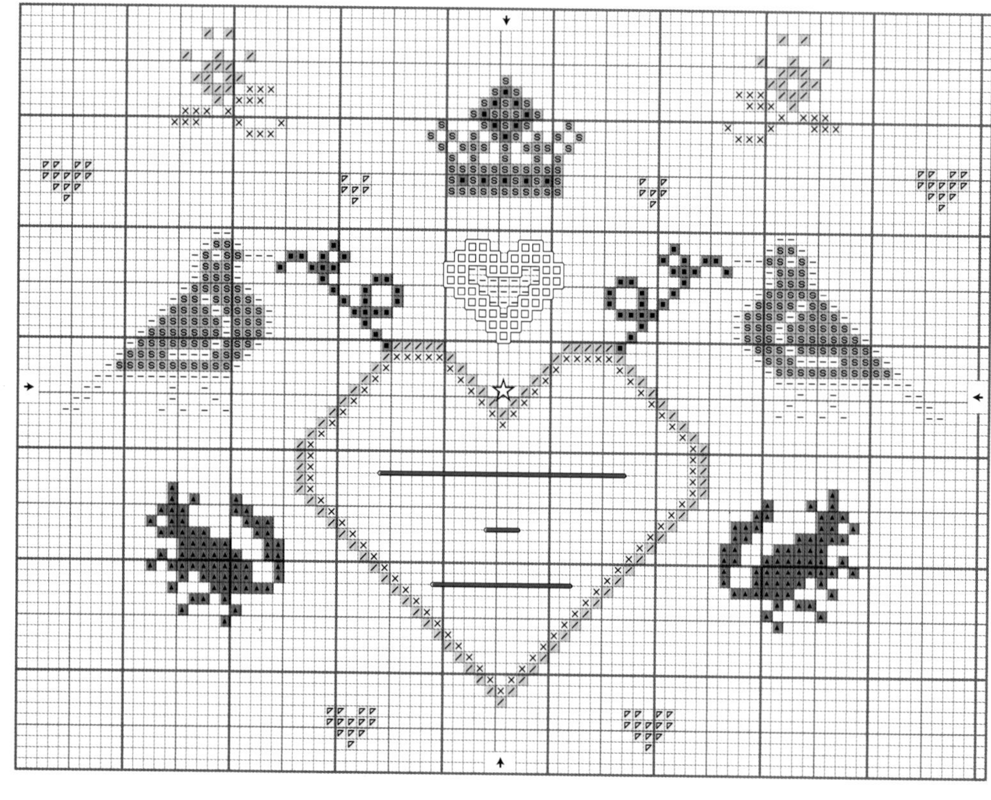

Oval Birth Sampler

X X DMC stranded cotton (floss) ecru

◸ ◸ DMC stranded cotton (floss) 3823 pale cream

▲ ▲ DMC stranded cotton (floss) 948 very pale pink

– – DMC Flower thread blanc

■ ■ DMC Flower thread 2407 beige

Four-sided stitch surrounding heart – DMC stranded cotton (floss) 948 very pale pink

Name – DMC Flower thread 2407 beige tent stitch over 1 thread

S S Marlitt 1012 cream

/ / Marlitt 800 white

All tiny hearts worked in satin stitch using DMC stranded cotton (floss) 3823 pale cream

Large birds and crown infill with tent stitch using Marlitt 1012

Position name on ▬▬ line

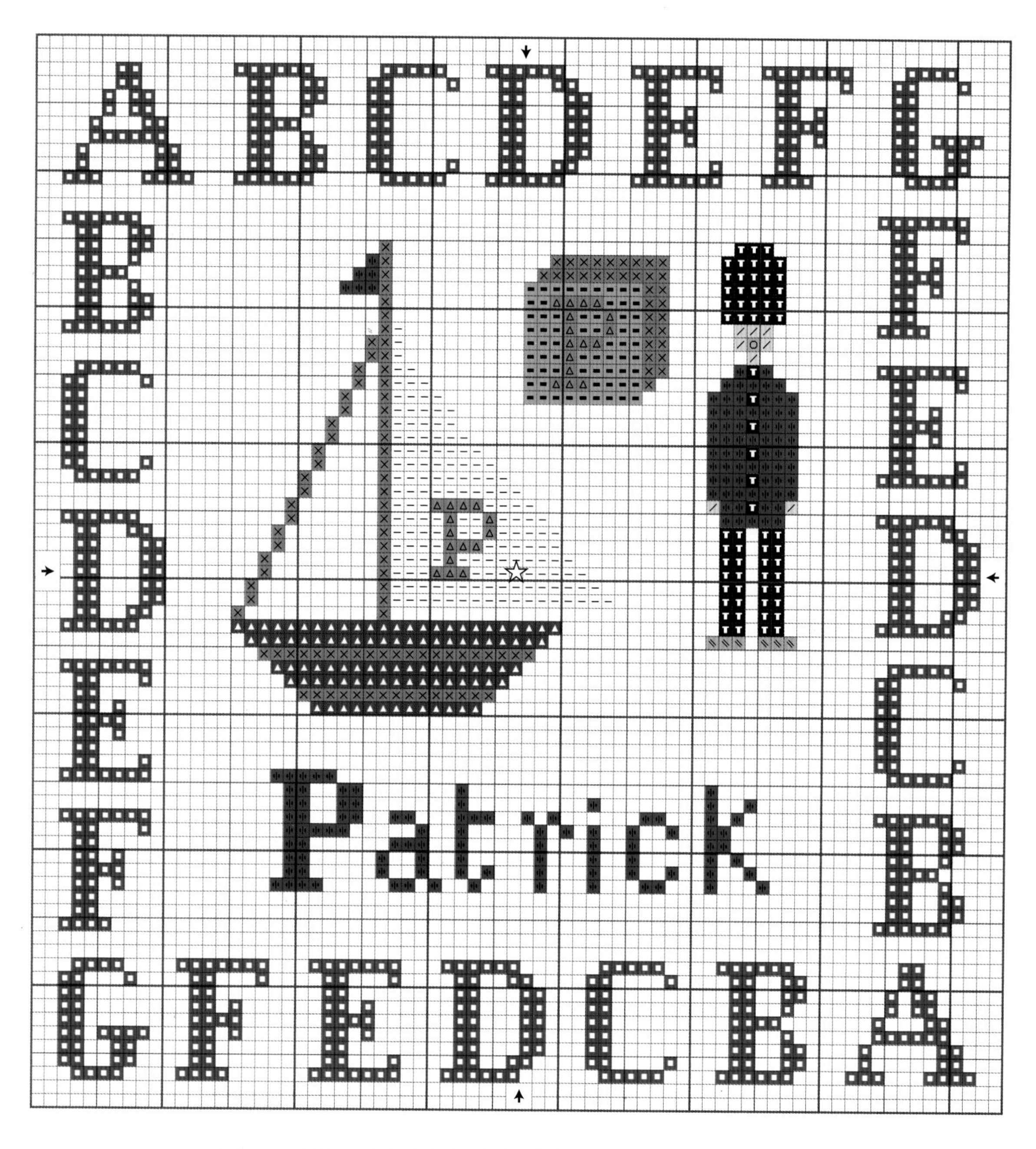

Boy's Name Picture

DMC

- 310 black
- 317 dark grey
- ecru
- 3371 dark brown
- 434 warm brown
- 680 gold
- 823 navy
- 347 red
- 407 pink beige
- 501 green blue
- 842 flesh

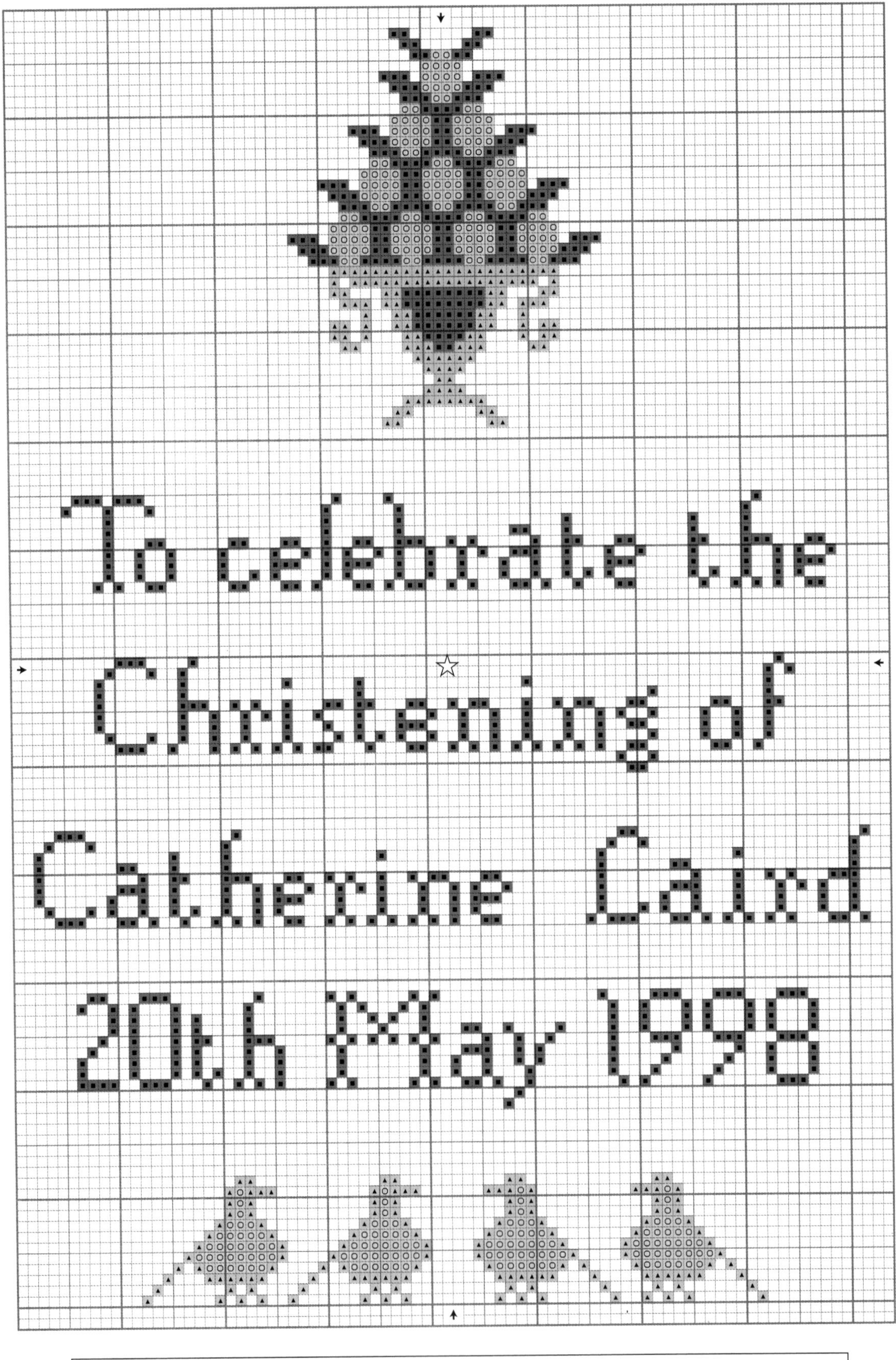
To celebrate the
Christening of
Catherine Caird
20th May 1998

Small Christening Sampler
DMC
926 dark slate blue
842 beige
927 pale slate blue

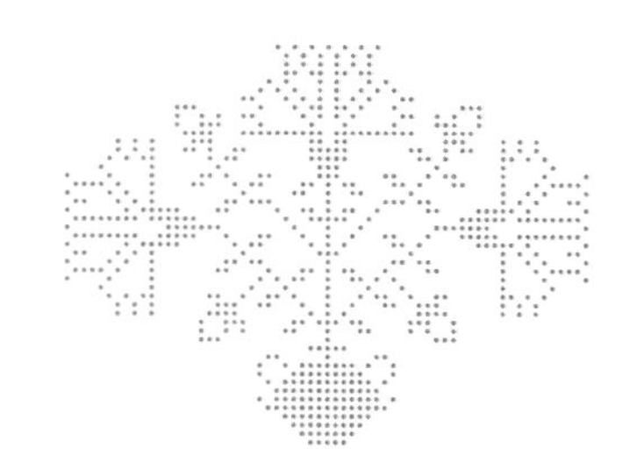

Additional Alphabets

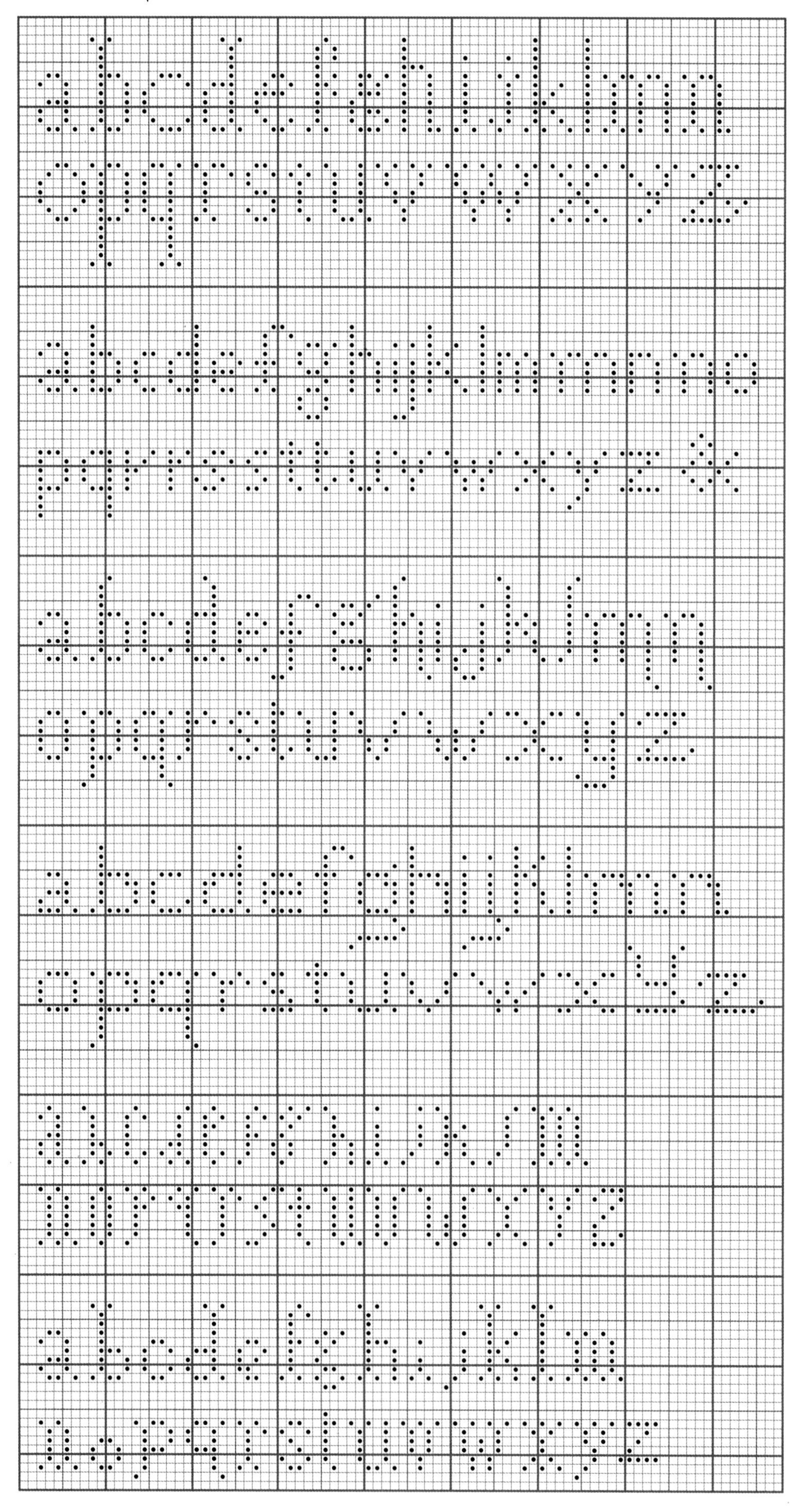

FINISHING TECHNIQUES

Mounts

Almost all work can be improved with the addition of one or two carefully chosen mounts (the exceptions being samplers which were traditionally close framed). In this instance, we are talking about cardboard mounts cut with a 45° angle to frame the work, not fabric covered ones which are mentioned later in the chapter. No instructions are given for cutting your own card mounts because I would very strongly advise against this. Just like plastering a wall, unless you are aiming for that 'rough-cast' look, leave it to the experts. It is possible to buy special tools for cutting mounts, but the old adage 'you get what you pay for' certainly applies here and the cheaper versions (in my humble opinion) are not worth the box they are housed in. Unless you intend to take up picture framing seriously, then it simply isn't worth buying expensive equipment that you will seldom use. Mounts always look better if they are professionally cut with a 45° angle and most picture framers will be happy to do this. A double mount invariably looks better than a single one and will add depth and interest to your work.

Take your time choosing the colours as this is a vital part of the finishing process. An easy way to achieve success is to match the colours as closely as possible to those which appear in the design. Consider also using mounts with a shaped aperture. Consult your picture framer first however. I once requested a heart-shaped mount and was presented with eleven rejected pieces of card with badly cut hearts, one unimpressive finished model, a very exasperated framer and a very large bill – *not* the framer I use now, I hasten to add! Round, oval, triangular and similar shaped mounts should prove no problem however and there are framers around who specialise in extremely complicated and very beautifully cut mounts (see Suppliers page 143).

Framing Your Work

Traditionally, samplers were close framed – that is, framed without a card mount – in woods such as maple, cherry or rosewood. If you are aiming for a totally traditional look, then this is the path you should follow. For more modern versions of sampler design however, there is no need to stick rigidly to this rule. Some light and pretty birth or anniversary samplers (see Little Girls Sampler page 126) look even better with the addition of a carefully chosen mount.

It is always worth taking your finished work to a professional framer. The correct choice of frame can quite simply make or break a piece of work. You may have spent many hours on the embroidery, so it would be sacrilege at this stage to spoil it with an inappropriate frame.

Unless your work is very textured, the use of glass is advisable as it protects the work from dust, dirt, insects and inquisitive fingers. (You will find that almost everyone has an irresistible urge to run their fingers over your work!) Your framer will probably ask you to choose between plain and non-reflective glass. Non-reflective glass certainly sounds the obvious choice, but in actuality it has a flat rather mottled appearance which tends to dull colours. Plain glass will show your work to much better advantage. If you have decided to use glass but are not using a mount, ask your picture framer to use thin strips of card to prevent the glass coming into contact with the needlework to stop it from flattening the stitches.

Before taking your embroidery to the framers or framing it yourself, check the following list:

❊ Check the completed design against the chart. It's so easy to miss out stitches or even whole areas of the design.

❊ Turn your work over and check for loose trailing threads. Check that the threads are secure, then snip them off as close to the work as possible. Dark-coloured trailing threads in particular will show through light fabric and spoil the appearance of the finished work.

❋ If you have to launder your work, wash it gently by hand with mild soap flakes (or embroidery shampoo which is now available from needlework shops), taking great care not to rub or wring. Simply swish the embroidery about in the water. Rinse well then roll in a clean white towel. Open out and leave to dry. To press, lay several layers of towelling on an ironing-board. Lay the work face down on the towels, cover with a clean white cloth and press with a warm iron. This method prevents the stitches from becoming flattened. Do not iron canvas or perforated paper.

Stretching, Blocking And Mounting Your Work

This part of the finishing process is vital (unless your embroidery is very tiny indeed), as the most wonderful piece of work can be totally ruined if it is puckered or creased. It is a simple procedure to master, but if your work is to be professionally framed, your framer will be able to do this for you.

Strong acid-free mount board (available from good art shops), or hardboard (usually only for larger pieces of work) covered with acid-free paper
Pins
Strong thread, such as crochet cotton
Needle

1 Measure your work and then cut the mount board slightly bigger than your embroidery if a mount is to be used, or, if not, to the size of your chosen frame.

2 Place the card or covered hardboard on the wrong side of the embroidery and when in position secure with straight pins inserted into the edge (Fig 1). Turn frequently to check that the embroidery remains correctly placed.

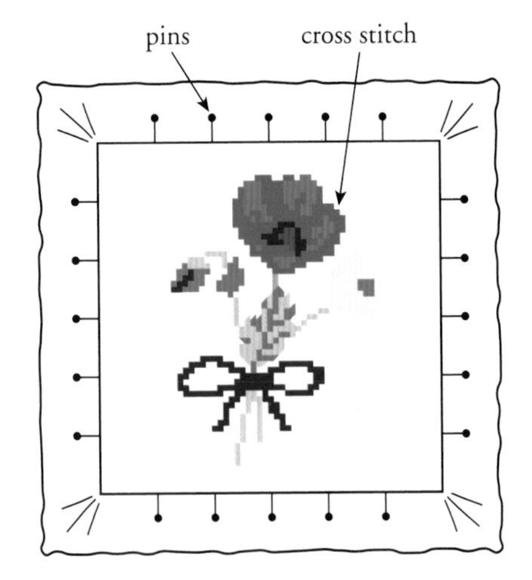

Fig 1 Stretching Linen or Aida Fabric.

3 Fold over the side edges of the fabric, then use a long length of strong thread to lace back and forth (Fig 2a). Pull up the stitches to tighten and secure firmly.

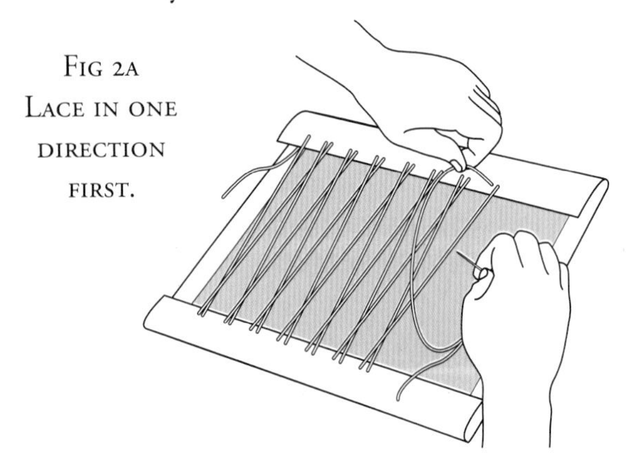

Fig 2a Lace in one direction first.

4 Complete the top and bottom sides in the same way (Fig 2b).

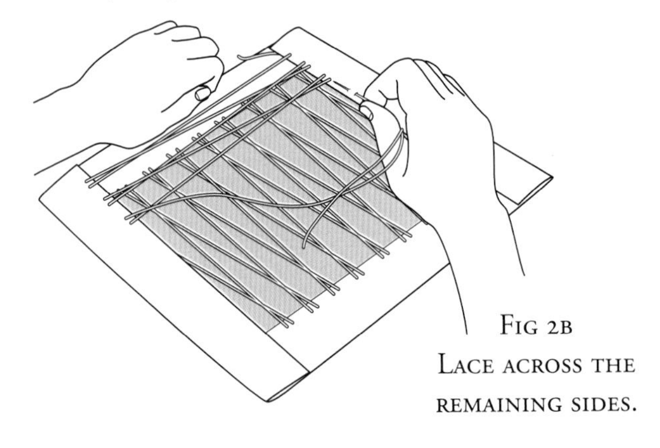

Fig 2b Lace across the remaining sides.

Blocking (or Stretching) Canvas Work

If you have not used a frame (or sometimes even if you have), canvas work can become badly distorted and will need stretching back into shape.

A thick wooden board, larger than your embroidery and soft enough to take drawing pins or tacks
Several sheets of newspaper or blotting paper
Plain white porous paper on which you have drawn the outline size of your embroidery in waterproof pen
Brass drawing pins or tacks
For further materials needed for mounting your canvas work, see the listing for Stretching and Blocking as before (page 138)

1 Lay the sheets of paper on the wooden board and wet them thoroughly; a plant sprayer is ideal. On top of this lay the sheet of white paper with the size of your design marked on it.

2 Lay the embroidery right side up centrally on top of this. Then, starting at the top centre, insert the drawing pins at intervals of approximately 1in (2.5cm), working outwards and stretching the canvas as you go. Pin along the bottom edge in the same way and then the sides (Fig 3).

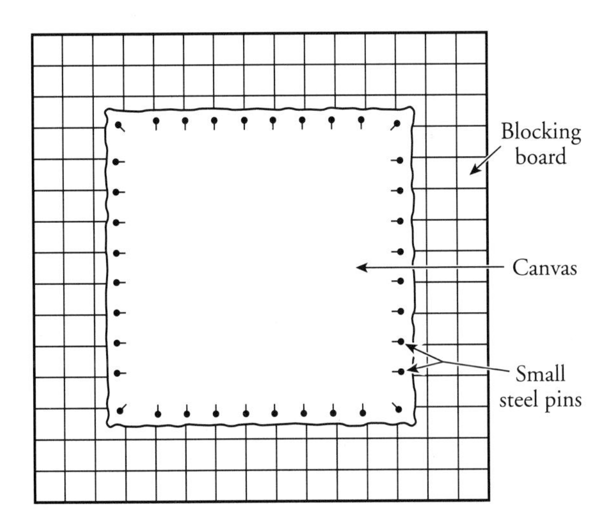

Fig 3 Place the embroidery on a wooden board and pin at regular intervals.

3 Leave the canvas to dry thoroughly – this could take as long as two or three days. If the canvas was badly distorted, it may be necessary to repeat the whole process.

Fabric-Covered Mounts

By covering a mount with fabric you need not restrict yourself to a plain, uninteresting mount that does not do justice to your work. Virtually any colour, pattern or texture is possible with this method, and you could even add embroidery to match your design.

Strong card
Fabric
Glue or impact adhesive
Metal rule
Scalpel or craft knife
Cutting board or several layers of card to protect your working surface
For a padded mount, one or two layers of Terylene wadding (batting)

1 Measure the completed embroidery carefully and cut the mount and aperture to the size required. Round, oval and heart-shaped apertures are very difficult to cut perfectly and, even though you are covering with fabric, uneven edges will show. Unless you are very skilled, it is best if your picture framer cuts these for you.

2 Cut the fabric to the size of the mount, plus allowances for turnings. The allowance will vary according to the size of the mount and also the type of fabric (for example, because of its thickness, velvet will need a larger allowance than fine cotton). Always make sure that you align the mount with the straight grain of the fabric.

3 Place the fabric right side down and position the mount in the middle. If making a padded mount, cut the padding to the same size as the mount and place between the fabric and the card. Snip off the corners of the fabric as shown by the dotted lines in Fig 4a overleaf.

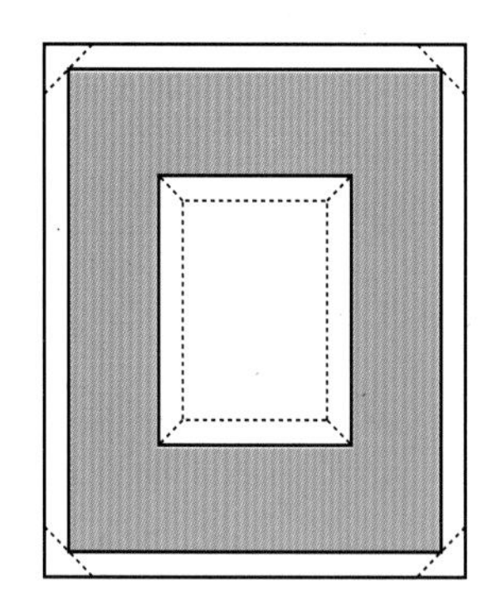

Fig 4a Position the mount over your fabric.

4 Apply adhesive to the remaining fabric at the outer edge. Fold over and press flat.

5 To cut the inside 'window', first cut out the rectangle as shown by the dotted lines in Fig 4a and carefully snip into the corners, stopping just short of the edge. Apply adhesive to this remaining fabric, fold over and press flat (Fig 4b).

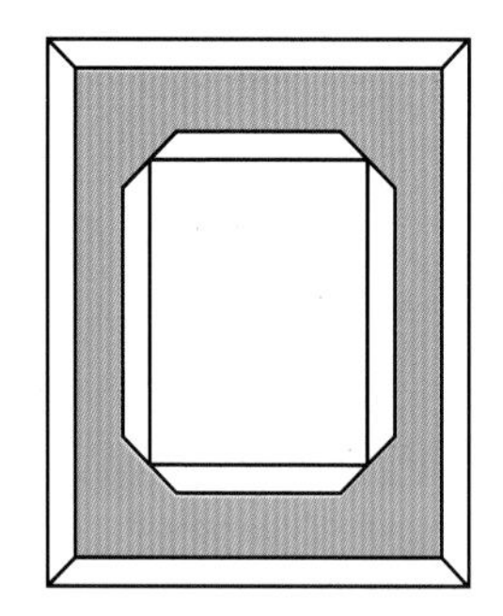

Fig 4b Fold back the inside edges of the fabric.

6 Apply any further embellishments you like – bows, braids and so on – and then carefully align the mount over the embroidery. Fix with glue or masking tape.

Charting Your Own House

One of the nicest parts of sampler making must surely be the personalising of this type of needlework and the realisation that future generations will be able to study it and gain some insight into our lives. One way to ensure that this happens (if you are not happy with designing an entire sampler), is to substitute some of the elements with your own details. Your name, date and dwelling place for example.

If you wish to substitute part of a design – your own house say for one of the houses shown in any of the samplers – this is easy to achieve. A word of caution however, a sixties-style house for example, is going to look a little incongruous set amongst traditional motifs, so substitute with care.

Size will also have to be taken into account. If you have a very large house, want all the details to show, and the house you are replacing is considerably smaller, you may have to work over just one thread of linen even if the rest of the design is worked over two. Another option, is to work a smaller version of your chosen design, using your own house, a border and a few of the motifs taken from the sampler. The following steps will help you to make a chart of your home.

1 Take a good colour photograph of your home, face on. If necessary, enlarge the design on a photocopier to the size you wish the finished work to be. There are now many shops that offer this facility.

2 Place a sheet of tracing graph paper over the design. This is available in various counts which correspond to the fabric thread count, so, if for example, you wish to work on 28 count linen over two threads (or 14 count Aida), choose 14 count tracing graph paper. Remember to take into account that if you are working on linen you will most likely be working over two threads, so simply halve the number of threads of linen to obtain the tracing paper count. Trace the design on to the graph paper, squaring up the design and eliminating any unnecessary details.

3 Colour in the design using coloured crayons. If you have a manufacturer's shade card, match the colours to the shade numbers. The chart is now ready to stitch from.

4 Check that the design will fit the available space if you are replacing a house on a sampler. Or, if you are creating an additional design using elements from a larger work, position your house on a larger chart and add your border, motifs etc.

Making a Twisted Cord

1 Assess the length of cord you require and then cut a length of thread which is three times as long.

2 Make a loop in each end of the thread and then attach one end to a hook or doorknob (Fig 5a).

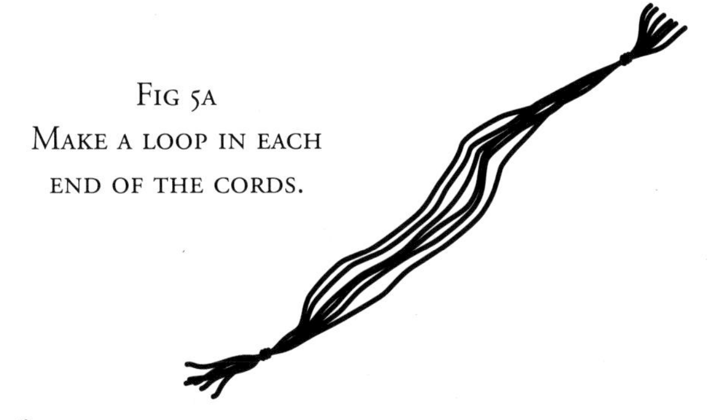

Fig 5a
Make a loop in each end of the cords.

3 Slip a pencil through the other end and, keeping the thread taut, begin twisting the pencil round and round until, when it is released, the thread begins to twist back on itself (Fig 5b).

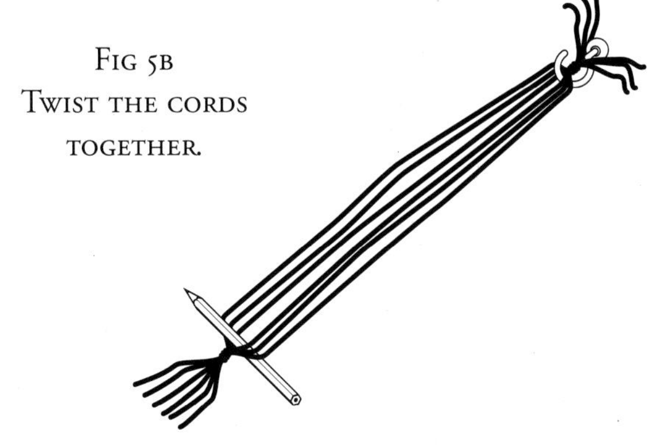

Fig 5b
Twist the cords together.

4 Keeping the threads taut, fold the twisted length in half, matching the ends together (Fig 5c). Stroke along the cord to even out the twists. Finally, tie the ends together. If a thicker cord is required, simply use more strands of thread initially.

Fig 5c
Fold the cord in half.

Making a Fold-Over Card

An enormous variety of ready-made fold-over cards are now available from art and needlework shops but if the size or colour you want is not available you can easily make your own.

Thin card in your chosen colour
Craft knife
Glue or double-sided adhesive tape

1 Measure your embroidery to assess the size and shape of the aperture but remember that round, oval and heart-shaped apertures are much more difficult to cut accurately unless you have great skill. Do not attempt to cut any aperture with scissors: always use a craft knife or scalpel.

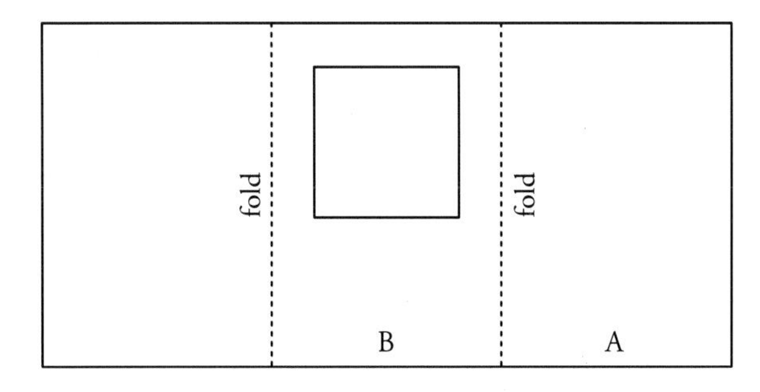

Fig 6a Cut your card to the required shape.

2 Cut your card to the size and shape required (Fig 6a). Cut an aperture in the middle section 'B' and, using a craft knife, lightly score fold lines as indicated by the dotted lines.

3 Position the aperture over your embroidery. Trim away any excess fabric and glue into position or secure with double-sided adhesive tape.

4 Fold section 'A' over section 'B' and glue these firmly together (Fig 6b).

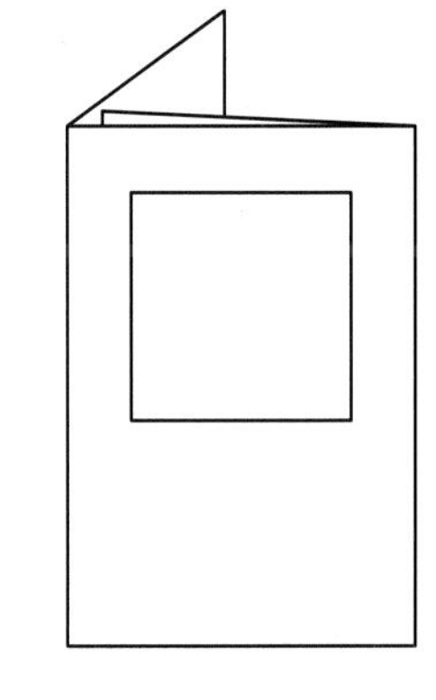

Fig 6b Fold and glue the sections into place.

Making up a Cushion

Your completed piece of embroidery
Piece of backing fabric 1in (2.5cm) larger all round than the finished embroidery
Matching sewing thread
Zip long enough for one side (optional)
Cushion pad
Twisted cord to edge (or see page 141)

1 If your finished embroidery is not quite straight, block (damp stretch) it (see page 139).

2 Trim the canvas to within ¾in (2cm) of the embroidery, cutting across the corners diagonally to within ¼in (0.5cm) to reduce bulk and create a neater finish.

3 Pin and tack (baste) the embroidery and backing fabric with right sides together, trimming backing fabric to size. Machine or hand stitch together, leaving a large enough gap on the fourth side to take the cushion pad. Oversew or zigzag the seams to strengthen them.

4 If you have chosen to insert a zip, add it at this stage. Alternatively, turn the cushion right side out, insert the pad and close with small invisible stitches.

5 Sew the twisted cord by hand to the edge of the cushion where the embroidery meets the backing fabric using a matching thread. Bind the edges of the cord with masking tape until ready to sew them to the cushion, making sure you stitch them down firmly as they tend to unravel quickly.

Making up a Pincushion

Piece of backing fabric 1in (2.5cm) larger all round than the finished embroidery
Matching sewing thread
Terylene wadding (batting) for filling
Twisted cord to edge (or see page 141)

Follow instructions for making up a cushion (above), ignoring advice about the zip and cushion pad and fill instead with the Terylene wadding (batting).

Bibliography

Bridgeman, Harriet and Drury, Elizabeth, *Needlework*, Paddington Press Ltd. (1978)

Cirker, Blanche (Ed), *Needlework Alphabets and Designs*, Dover (1975)

Clabburn, Pamela, *The Needleworker's Dictionary*, Macmillan (1976)

Colby, Averil, *Samplers*, Batsford (1964)

Crawford, Heather M., *Needlework Samplers of Northern Ireland*, Allingham Publishing (1989)

Deforges, R. and Dormann, G., *Alphabets*, Albin Mitchel (1987)

Don, Sarah, *Traditional Samplers*, David & Charles (1986)

Edmonds, Mary Jaene, *Samplers and Samplermakers (An American Schoolgirl Art 1700–1850)*, Rizzoli International Publications, Inc. (1991)

Eirwen Jones, Mary, *British Samplers*, Batsford (1948)

The Embroiderers' Guild Practical Library, *Making Samplers*, David & Charles (1993)

Fawdry, Marguerite and Brown, Deborah, *The Book of Samplers*, Lutterworth Press (1980)

Forstner, Regina, *Traditional Samplers*, Rosenheimer Verlaghaus Alfred Forh GmbH & Co. (1983)

Hersh, Tandy and Charles, *Samplers of the Pennsylvania Germans*, The Pennsylvania German Society (1991)

Huish, Marcus, *Samplers and Tapestry Embroideries*, Dover (1970)

Jenkins, Mary, *House & Garden Samplers*, David & Charles (1996)

Kay, Dorothea, *Sew a Sampler*, A & C Black Ltd. (1979)

Keyes, Brenda, *The Sampler Motif Book*, David & Charles (1995)

LaBranche, John F. and Conant, Rita F., *In Female Worth and Elegance*, The Portsmouth Marine Society (1996)

Lammer, Jutta, *Making Samplers (New & Traditional Designs)*, Sterling Publishing Co. Inc. (1984)

Lewis, Felicity, *Needlepoint Samplers*, Studio Vista (1981)

Mayor, Susan and Fowle, Diana, *Samplers*, Studio Editions Ltd (1990)

Meulenbelt-Nieuwburg, Alberta, *Embroidery Motifs from Dutch Samplers*, Batsford (1974)

O'Steen, Darlene, *The Proper Stitch, Symbol of Excellence* Publishers, Inc. (1994)

Pesel, Louisa F. *Historical Designs for Embroidery*, Dover (1970)

Ring, Betty, *American Needlework Treasures*, E. P. Dutton (1987)

Ring, Betty, *American Samplers and Pictorial Needlework, 1650–1850 Girlhood Embroidery (Vols I & II)*, Alfred A. Knopf, Inc. (1993)

Ryan, Patricia and Bragdon, Allen D., *Historic Samplers*, Bullfinch Press (1992)

Sebba, Anne, *Samplers: Five Centuries of a Gentle Craft*, Thames & Hudson (1979)

Stanwood Bolton, Ethel and Johnson Coe, Eve, *American Samplers*, Dover (1973)

Stevens, Christine, *Samplers (From the Welsh Folk Museum Collection)*, Gomer Press (1991)

Synge, Lanto, *The Royal School of Needlework Book of Needlework and Embroidery*, Wm Collins Sons & Co. Ltd. (1986)

Van Valin, Marsha, *Alphabets from Early Samplers*, The Scarlet Letter (1994)

Museums, Art Galleries and Other Places of Interest

It is advisable to telephone first for full addresses, opening hours and to make sure that the collections are open for viewing.

The American Museum in Britain, Bath, Tel: 01225 460503

City of Bristol Museum and Art Gallery, Bristol, Tel: 01272 223571

The Burrell Collection, Glasgow, Tel: 0141 649 7151

Buckinghamshire County Museum, Aylesbury, Bucks, Tel: 01296 331441

Fitzwilliam Museum, Cambridge, Tel: 01223 332900

Gawthorpe Hall, Burnley, Lancashire, Tel: 01282 771004

Guildford Museum, Guildford, Tel: 01483 444750

Hove Museum and Art Gallery, East Sussex, Tel: 01273 290200

Montacute House, Montacute, Somerset, Tel: 01935 823289

Rufford Old Hall, Rufford, Lancashire, Tel: 01704 821254

Wells Museum, Wells, Somerset, Tel: 01749 673477

Whitby Museum, Whitby, North Yorkshire, Tel: 01947 602908

Whitworth Art Gallery, Manchester, Tel: 0161 2757452

Witney Antiques, Witney, Oxon, Tel: 01993 703902

Victoria and Albert Museum, London, Tel: 0171 938 8500

Suppliers

Craft Creations, 1–7 Harper's Yard, Ruskin Road, Tottenham, London N17 8NE.
Greetings cards with pre-cut mounts.
DMC Creative World, Pullman Road, Wigston, Leicester LE18 2DY.
Zweigart fabrics and DMC threads.
Framecraft Ltd., 372–376 Summer Lane, Hockley, Birmingham B19 3QA.
Trinket pots and wedding rings.
Macleod Craft Marketing, West Yonderton, Warlock Road, Bridge of Weir, Renfrewshire PA11 3SR.
For list of stockists of the Caron Watercolours threads collection.
R&R Enterprises, 13 Frederick Road, Malvern, Worcs WR14 1RS.
Plastic easy-lock frames.
Siesta Bar Frames, P.O. Box 1759, Ringwood, Hants BH24 3XN.
Willow Fabrics, 27 Willow Green, Knutsford, Cheshire WA16 6AX.
Linen and Aida fabrics.

General Needlecraft Suppliers (with a mail order facility)
When writing to any of the following suppliers, please include a stamped self-addressed envelope for your reply.

Campden Needlecraft, High Street, Chipping Campden, Gloucestershire GL55 6AG.
Voirrey Embroidery, Brimstage Hall, Brimstage, Wirral, Cheshire L63 6JA.
Wye Needlecraft, 2 Royal Oak Place, Matlock Street, Bakewell, Derbyshire DE45 1HD.

The Sampler Company

Brenda Keyes sampler charts, complete kits and 'Country Yarns' Thread Organisers are available from selected needlecraft shops, and also from:
The Sampler Company, Holly Tree House, Lichfield Drive, Prestwich, Manchester M25 OHX. Please write for details or telephone/fax 0161 773 9330.

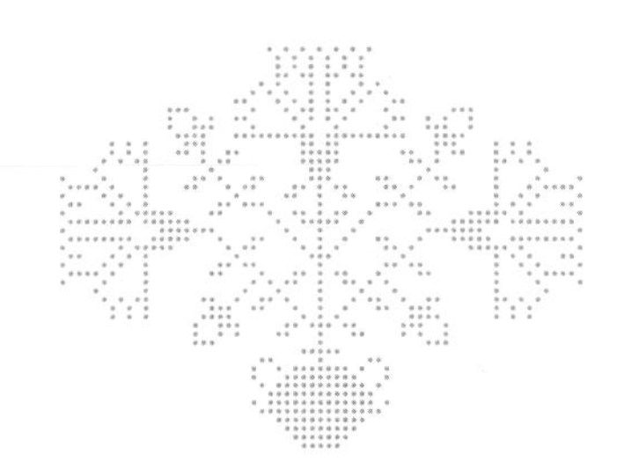

Index

Numbers in *italic* indicate illustrations